.CLASSIC.

CONNECTICUT

.CUISINE.

CONNECTICUT
EASTER SEALS

Easter Seals
®

Mark Johnson is an artist from the shoreline town of Branford, Connecticut. A lifelong love of Long Island Sound is reflected in many of his scenes. In this painting, two children collect treasures, with Branford's Thimble Islands in the background.

This cookbook is a collection of favorite recipes, which are not necessarily original recipes.

Published by The Easter Seal Society of Connecticut, Inc.

Library of Congress Catalog Number: 94-71856
ISBN: 0-87197-406-1

Edited, Designed and Manufactured by
Favorite Recipes© Press
P.O. Box 305142
Nashville, Tennessee 37230
1-800-358-0560

Manufactured in the United States of America
First Printing: 1994   10,000 copies

Credits

Cookbook Committee Chairmen

Noreen Aresco
The Easter Seal Rehabilitation Center of Central Connecticut

Jerry D'Achille
Easter Seals Camp Hemlocks

Betsie Dougherty and Sharon Ewen
Easter Seal Goodwill Industries Rehabilitation Center
of New Haven

Michael Jubinsky
The Easter Seal Rehabilitation Center of Southeastern Connecticut

Susan Ponton
The Easter Seal Rehabilitation Center of Greater Waterbury

Cover

Mark Johnson
Branford

Photographers

Dolores Conte
Guilford

Ernest J. Larsen, Jr.
Meriden

Georgia Sheron
Oakville

Connecticut Department of Economic Development
Essex Steam Train and Riverboat
Mystic Seaport
SNET

Contents

Contents

*E*aster Seals of Connecticut has been a vital resource, meeting the needs of people with disabilities throughout communities in our state, since 1935. The organization continues to fulfill its commitment to assist children and adults with disabilities achieve maximum independence, by providing speech, occupational, physical therapy and vocational rehabilitation services.

The Connecticut Easter Seal network has grown to include six outpatient rehabilitation centers located in Hartford, Meriden, New Haven, Stamford, Uncasville and Waterbury, as well as a barrier-free, year-round camping facility at Camp Hemlocks in Hebron.

Through integrated rehabilitation services, technological assistance, disability prevention, advocacy, and public education programs, Easter Seals empowers people to reach their maximum potential.

All proceeds from the sale of each cookbook will be used exclusively by Easter Seals in Connecticut to provide direct services for people with disabilities.

·CLASSIC·
CONNECTICUT
·CUISINE·

APPETIZERS
& BEVERAGES

LIGHTHOUSE POINT • NEW HAVEN

Spring Antipasto

3/4 cup olive oil
2 teaspoons chopped
  parsley
1 teaspoon thyme
Salt and pepper to taste
4 (2¹/₂-inch) rounds of
  goat cheese
1 cup fine bread crumbs
Terrine of Eggplant
  (below)
Vegetable Chili (page 9)
Grilled Shiitake
  Mushrooms (page 9)
4 (2-ounce) pieces thinly
  sliced prosciutto
4 figs (optional)
Basil oil
Italian parsley

- Combine olive oil, chopped parsley, thyme, salt and pepper in bowl; mix well. Add cheese. Marinate for 1 hour.
- Coat cheese with bread crumbs; place in lightly oiled baking dish. Bake at 400 degrees for 6 minutes.
- Place cheese on radicchio leaf in center of 10-inch plate. Arrange Terrine of Eggplant, Vegetable Chili, Grilled Shiitake Mushrooms, prosciutto and figs around cheese. Sprinkle with basil oil and Italian parsley.
- This recipe is from Michael J. Bonanno, Jr., Banquet Chef of the Foxwood Casino.
- Yield: 12 servings.

Terrine of Eggplant

2 medium eggplant, sliced
  lengthwise
2 to 3 cups olive oil
2 medium onions, sliced
1 tablespoon chopped
  garlic
1 bunch basil, chopped
Salt and pepper to taste
6 red bell peppers,
  roasted, peeled, cut into
  halves
4 ounces mozzarella
  cheese, sliced

- Sauté eggplant several slices at a time in part of the olive oil in large sauté pan until golden brown on both sides, adding olive oil as needed. Remove and drain eggplant.
- Sauté onions, garlic and basil in pan until light brown. Season with salt and pepper.
- Alternate layers of eggplant, peppers, onion mixture and cheese in terrine pan until all ingredients are used.
- Bake at 350 degrees for 8 to 10 minutes.
- Yield: 10 to 12 servings.

Vegetable Chili

1 each large red and green
  bell pepper, finely
  chopped
Olive oil
1 cup frozen corn, thawed
Salt and pepper to taste
2 medium Spanish onions,
  chopped
6 cloves of garlic, chopped
1 (35-ounce) can Italian
  plum tomatoes, chopped
1/3 cup olive oil
1 tablespoon chili powder
1 1/4 tablespoons oregano
2 teaspoons cumin
1 teaspoon cayenne pepper
1 cup kidney beans
1 cup chickpeas
1 cup cannellini beans
8 ounces snow peas, cut
  into 1/4-inch pieces

- Sauté bell peppers in olive oil in sauté pan for 2 to 3 minutes. Add corn, salt and pepper.
- Simmer onions, garlic and tomatoes in 1/3 cup olive oil in large saucepan over medium heat. Stir in chili powder, oregano, cumin, salt and cayenne pepper. Add pepper mixture, kidney beans, chickpeas, cannellini beans and snow peas. Adjust seasonings.
- Yield: 8 servings.

Grilled Shiitake Mushrooms

16 medium shiitake
  mushrooms
2 tablespoons chopped
  garlic
1/4 to 1/2 cup olive oil
1 tablespoon chopped
  parsley
2 teaspoons thyme
Salt and pepper to taste

- Combine mushrooms with garlic, olive oil, parsley, thyme, salt and pepper in small bowl; mix gently. Marinate for 20 minutes.
- Grill mushrooms for 8 to 10 minutes.
- Yield: 4 servings.

Antipasto

2 small jars marinated
 artichokes, chopped
2 pints marinated
 mushrooms
1 jar pepper salad
2 cans pitted black olives,
 drained
1 can chickpeas, drained
1 small link pepperoni,
 thinly sliced
1 jar large stuffed hot
 peppers, drained
2 jars Tuscan peppers,
 drained
1 jar cauliflower, drained
Oregano to taste
4 (1/2-inch thick) slices
 Genoa salami, cubed
4 (1/2-inch thick) slices
 Provolone cheese, cubed
1 or 2 pints cherry
 tomatoes
1 can anchovies (optional)

- Combine artichokes, mushrooms and pepper salad with their marinade in large bowl. Add olives, chickpeas, pepperoni, hot peppers, Tuscan peppers, cauliflower and oregano in large bowl. Chill overnight or up to several days.
- Add salami, cheese, tomatoes and anchovies; mix gently.
- This was served at former Congressman William Ratchford's inauguration party.
- Yield: 15 servings.

Artichoke Bars

2 (6-ounce) jars
 marinated artichoke
 hearts
1 large onion, chopped
1 clove of garlic, chopped
4 eggs
1/2 cup seasoned bread
 crumbs
2 tablespoons chopped
 parsley
1/2 teaspoon oregano
1/4 teaspoon pepper
8 ounces sharp Cheddar
 cheese, shredded

- Drain and chop artichokes, reserving marinade from 1 jar.
- Sauté onion and garlic in reserved marinade in skillet until tender.
- Beat eggs in large bowl. Add bread crumbs, parsley, oregano and pepper; mix well. Stir in cheese, sautéed onion mixture and artichokes.
- Spoon into 7x11-inch baking dish. Bake at 350 degrees for 30 minutes. Cut into bars. Serve warm or cooled.
- Yield: 16 servings.

Bacon Squares

1 cup mayonnaise
1 tablespoon horseradish
  sauce
2 teaspoons
  Worcestershire sauce
1/2 teaspoon salad
  seasoning
1/4 teaspoon paprika
2 cups shredded Cheddar
  cheese
8 slices bacon, crisp-fried,
  crumbled
4 green onions, sliced
14 slices white bread

• Combine mayonnaise, horseradish
  sauce, Worcestershire sauce, salad
  seasoning and paprika in bowl; mix
  well. Stir in cheese, bacon and green
  onions.
• Spread about 3 tablespoons bacon
  mixture on each slice of bread; place on
  ungreased baking sheet.
• Bake at 400 degrees for 10 minutes. Cut
  each slice into 4 pieces. Serve hot.
• Yield: 56 servings.

Brie in a Blanket

1 (4-count) can crescent
  rolls
1 small wheel Brie cheese
2 tablespoons favorite
  jelly, jam or relish

• Unroll dough. Press edges and
  perforations to seal to form square.
• Cut cheese horizontally into 2 layers.
  Place 1 layer in center of dough. Spread
  with jelly and top with remaining cheese.
• Pull up dough to enclose cheese
  completely, pressing edges to seal. Place
  on baking sheet.
• Bake at 400 degrees for 12 to 15 minutes
  or until golden brown. Let stand for 20
  minutes before serving. Top with
  additional jelly if desired.
• Yield: 8 servings.

Make a tasty spread for rye bread of bleu cheese, cottage
cheese, crisp bacon bits and sliced stuffed olives.

Brie Tart

1 unbaked (8-inch) pie
  shell
8 ounces Brie cheese
2 tablespoons whipping
  cream
2 eggs, beaten
1 teaspoon confectioners'
  sugar
1/2 teaspoon turmeric
1 teaspoon ginger
Salt and pepper to taste

- Bake pie shell at 425 degrees for 10 minutes. Reduce oven temperature to 375 degrees.
- Remove rind from cheese; cut into cubes. Melt cheese in double boiler. Stir in cream, egg, confectioners' sugar, turmeric, ginger, salt and pepper.
- Spoon into pie shell. Bake at 375 degrees for 30 minutes or until light brown. Serve hot or cooled.
- Yield: 6 servings.

Cheese and Peppers

1 small green bell pepper
1 small red bell pepper
2 ounces Monterey Jack
  cheese, sliced, cut into
  strips

- Cut peppers into 1-inch strips. Arrange inner side up on plate sprayed with nonstick cooking spray. Place 1 strip cheese on each strip of pepper.
- Microwave on High for 1 1/4 to 1 1/2 minutes or until cheese is softened. Let stand for several minutes. Cut each pepper strip into 3 pieces, spooning cheese back onto peppers if necessary.
- Yield: 8 servings.

Vary dips by substituting yogurt for sour cream or Neufchâtel cheese for cream cheese. Cottage cheese processed in a blender until smooth and creamy can be substituted for either sour cream or yogurt to reduce calories.

Chard Tart

1 pound Swiss chard
1 pound onions, chopped
1 tablespoon butter
1½ pounds tomatoes,
    peeled, chopped, seeded
1 tablespoon butter
Nutmeg, salt and pepper
    to taste
1 unbaked (9-inch) tart
    shell
¼ to ⅓ pound Gruyère
    cheese, shredded

- Remove stems and thick ribs from chard; slice crosswise.
- Sauté onions in 1 tablespoon butter in skillet until tender but not brown. Add tomatoes. Cook until liquid has evaporated, stirring occasionally.
- Cook chard in 1 tablespoon butter in large skillet until wilted and most of the liquid has evaporated. Stir in nutmeg, salt and pepper.
- Line tart shell with foil and fill with dried beans, peach pits or tart weights. Bake at 425 degrees for 3 to 6 minutes. Remove weights and foil. Bake for 3 to 8 minutes longer or just until shell begins to brown.
- Layer half the tomato mixture, chard mixture, remaining tomato mixture and cheese in tart shell. Bake for 30 to 40 minutes or until golden brown. Serve warm or cooled. May bake for shorter time in tartlet shells if preferred.
- Yield: 6 servings.

Parmesan Chicken Wings

2 pounds chicken wings
¾ cup grated Parmesan
    cheese
2 tablespoons flour
1 tablespoon basil
¾ teaspoon salt
¼ cup milk
¼ cup melted margarine

- Rinse chicken wings and pat dry. Cut each wing into 3 portions, discarding tip portions.
- Combine cheese, flour, basil and salt in plastic bag. Dip chicken into milk. Shake several pieces at a time in cheese mixture, coating well.
- Place on greased baking sheet; drizzle with margarine. Bake at 400 degrees for 35 minutes, turning wings after 15 minutes.
- Yield: 8 servings.

Chicken Pillows

2 whole chicken breasts, skinned, boned, cut into halves
3 tablespoons lemon juice
3 tablespoons olive oil or vegetable oil
1 teaspoon minced garlic
1 teaspoon crumbled oregano
1/2 teaspoon salt
8 ounces phyllo or strudel pastry
1/2 cup melted butter

• Cut chicken into 1-inch cubes; rinse and pat dry. Combine with lemon juice, oil, garlic, oregano and salt in small bowl; mix well. Marinate in refrigerator overnight; drain.
• Place 1 sheet of phyllo pastry at a time on waxed paper, keeping remaining pastry covered to prevent drying out. Cut dough into halves lengthwise.
• Fold 1 strip into halves crosswise; brush with butter. Place 2 pieces of chicken at narrow end and roll pastry to midpoint to enclose chicken. Fold sides toward center and continue to roll pastry. Brush with butter and place seam side down on baking sheet.
• Repeat process with remaining pastry and chicken.
• Bake at 400 degrees for 15 minutes or until golden brown. May freeze prepared pillows and bake for 20 minutes.
• Yield: 24 servings.

Chili Cheese Squares

8 eggs
1/2 cup flour
1 teaspoon baking powder
3/4 teaspoon salt
3 cups shredded Monterey Jack cheese
1 1/2 cups cream-style cottage cheese
2 (4-ounce) cans chopped mild green chilies

• Beat eggs in mixer bowl for 4 to 5 minutes or until thick and lemon colored.
• Combine flour, baking powder and salt together. Add to eggs; mix well. Fold in cheeses and green chilies.
• Spoon into 9x13-inch baking dish. Bake at 350 degrees for 40 minutes. Let stand for 10 minutes. Cut into 2x2-inch squares. Serve warm or cooled.
• Yield: 24 servings.

Muenster Cheese Wedges

1 egg
3/4 cup flour
1 cup milk
1/2 teaspoon salt
1 cup shredded Muenster
   cheese

- Whisk egg lightly in bowl. Add flour and 1/2 cup milk. Whisk until smooth. Stir in remaining 1/2 cup milk and salt. Let stand for 1 hour.
- Stir in half the cheese. Spoon into greased 8-inch pie plate. Bake at 425 degrees for 30 minutes or until golden brown. Sprinkle with remaining cheese. Bake just until cheese melts. Cut into wedges.
- May freeze after first baking period if desired.
- Yield: 8 servings.

Phyllo Chilies Rellenos

2 (4-ounce) cans whole
   mild green chilies,
   drained
8 ounces phyllo pastry
Melted butter or
   extra-virgin olive oil
1 cup shredded Monterey
   Jack cheese
5 eggs
1/2 teaspoon cumin
1/4 teaspoon salt

- Rinse chilies in cold water and pat dry.
- Cut pastry sheets to fit square baking pan. Stack sheets and cover with plastic wrap or damp cloth to prevent drying out.
- Layer 8 sheets in baking pan, brushing each set lightly with butter. Layer chilies and cheese in prepared pan.
- Beat eggs with cumin and salt in bowl. Pour over layers. Top with 8 to 10 sheets of pastry, brushing each sheet with butter.
- Bake at 375 degrees for 35 minutes or until eggs are set and pastry is golden brown. Let stand for 15 minutes before serving.
- Yield: 20 to 26 servings.

Deli Delight

6 eggs
1/4 cup grated Parmesan cheese
2 (8-count) cans crescent rolls
8 ounces salami, chopped
8 ounces Provolone cheese, chopped
8 ounces cooked ham, chopped
2 small jars roasted sweet peppers, drained

- Beat eggs with Parmesan cheese in bowl.
- Line 9x13-inch baking dish with 1 can roll dough. Layer salami, Provolone cheese, ham, peppers and egg mixture 1/2 at a time in prepared dish. Top with second can of roll dough.
- Bake, covered with foil, at 375 degrees for 30 minutes. Bake, uncovered, until golden brown.
- This recipe was the appetizer winner of the Ellington Junior Womens Club's 1993 Recipe Contest.
- Yield: 32 servings.

Marinated Kielbasa

4 cloves of garlic, minced
3 tablespoons Dijon mustard
3/4 cup red wine vinegar
2 cups olive oil
2 tablespoons Italian seasoning
3 1/2 pounds kielbasa sausage
1 can small pitted black olives, drained
1 cup chopped scallions with tops
1/2 cup chopped parsley

- Combine garlic, mustard, vinegar, olive oil and Italian seasoning in blender container; process until smooth.
- Heat kielbasa in boiling water for 4 to 5 minutes; drain. Cut into 1/2-inch slices. Combine with olives, scallions and parsley in covered container.
- Add marinade; mix well. Marinate in refrigerator overnight, turning container several times.
- Spoon into glass dish. Microwave on High for 5 to 7 minutes or until heated through. Serve with wooden picks.
- Yield: 12 servings.

Make miniature pizzas on party breads,
English muffins, split pita rounds or bagels.

Bleu Cheese Deviled Ham Spirals

8 (6-inch) pita rounds
2/3 pound Saga bleu cheese,
 rind removed, softened
1/2 cup chopped walnuts
1/4 cup minced fresh
 parsley
1 1/2 tablespoons fresh
 lemon juice
1/4 teaspoon freshly
 ground white pepper
1 (6-ounce) cooked ham
 steak, trimmed, chopped
1/4 cup butter, softened
1 tablespoon honey
2 tablespoons Dijon
 mustard
1/4 teaspoon ground cloves
3 tablespoons coarse-
 ground mustard
1/3 cup minced fresh
 parsley
3 tablespoons chopped
 red onion
Black pepper to taste

- Split pita rounds horizontally. Stack between layers of dampened paper towels; cover with plastic wrap.
- Combine bleu cheese, walnuts, 1/4 cup parsley, lemon juice and white pepper in bowl; mix well with fork.
- Grind ham in food processor. Add butter, honey, Dijon mustard and cloves; process until smooth. Combine with coarse-ground mustard, 1/3 cup parsley, onion and black pepper in bowl; mix well.
- Spread bleu cheese mixture over inner side of half the pita rounds. Roll up pita round tightly to enclose filling; wrap with plastic wrap. Repeat with ham filling and remaining pita rounds. Chill rolls for 2 hours.
- Cut rolls crosswise into 1/4-inch slices with serrated knife. Arrange in decorative manner on serving plate; garnish with parsley sprigs.
- Yield: 80 servings.

Ham Cornucopias

1/2 cup mayonnaise
1 tablespoon milk
1/2 teaspoon prepared
 horseradish
1 large apple, chopped
1 medium stalk celery,
 sliced
1 (11-ounce) can
 mandarin oranges
1/2 cup chopped walnuts
1/2 cup flaked coconut
8 to 10 slices boiled ham
Parsley

- Combine mayonnaise, milk and horseradish in bowl. Add apple, celery, oranges, walnuts and coconut; mix lightly.
- Spread 1/3 cup apple mixture diagonally on each ham slice. Roll ham into cornucopias; secure with wooden picks. Serve on bed of parsley.
- Yield: 8 to 10 servings.

Oven-Fried Mushrooms

1/4 cup mayonnaise
1 tablespoon Dijon
  mustard or prepared
  horseradish
1 tablespoon chopped
  parsley
1/2 cup flour
1/2 teaspoon paprika
1 cup soft bread crumbs
1/2 cup grated Parmesan
  cheese
2 teaspoons crushed dried
  basil
2 eggs
2 tablespoons milk
16 ounces fresh
  mushrooms
1/4 cup melted butter or
  margarine

- Combine mayonnaise, mustard and parsley in small bowl; mix well. Set aside.
- Mix flour and paprika in plastic bag. Mix bread crumbs, cheese and basil in second plastic bag. Beat eggs with milk in bowl.
- Dip mushrooms into egg mixture. Shake in flour mixture and then in bread crumb mixture, pressing crumbs down gently.
- Arrange cap side down in lightly greased 10x15-inch baking pan; drizzle with butter.
- Bake at 450 degrees for 10 minutes or until golden brown. Serve with reserved sauce for dipping.
- Yield: 24 servings.

Pickled Mushrooms

6 tablespoons red wine
  vinegar
1/4 cup oil
1/4 teaspoon grated lemon
  rind
1/3 teaspoon parsley flakes
1/3 teaspoon thyme
1/8 teaspoon fennel seeds
1 bay leaf
1/2 teaspoon garlic powder
1 tablespoon salt
Pepper to taste
12 ounces fresh
  mushrooms
2 slices onion

- Combine vinegar, oil, lemon rind, parsley flakes, thyme, fennel seeds, bay leaf, garlic powder, salt and pepper in saucepan; mix well. Add mushrooms and onion.
- Bring to a boil; reduce heat. Simmer for 15 minutes.
- Spoon mixture into glass jar. Chill overnight or up to 2 days. Discard bay leaf before serving.
- Yield: 6 servings.

Mushroom Piroshki

9 ounces cream cheese,
 softened
1/2 cup butter, softened
1 1/2 cups flour
8 ounces mushrooms,
 minced
1 large onion, minced
3 tablespoons butter
1/4 teaspoon thyme
2 tablespoons flour
1 teaspoon salt
1/4 cup sour cream
1 egg, beaten

- Beat first 3 ingredients in large mixer bowl until soft dough forms. Chill for 1 hour or longer.
- Sauté mushrooms and onion in 3 tablespoons butter in skillet. Stir in thyme, 2 tablespoons flour, salt and sour cream. Chill in refrigerator.
- Roll dough into 2 very thin 15-inch circles on floured surface. Cut each into twenty 2 3/4-inch circles. Place 1 teaspoonful mushroom filling on each circle; brush edge with egg. Fold over to enclose filling, sealing edge and pricking top. Place on baking sheet; brush with egg. Chill in refrigerator.
- Bake, uncovered, at 450 degrees for 12 minutes or until brown. Serve hot.
- Yield: 40 servings.

Stuffed Mushrooms

20 large mushrooms
6 medium sweet Italian
 sausage links
1 medium onion, minced
3 or 4 cloves of garlic,
 minced
2 teaspoons olive oil
1 (10-ounce) package
 frozen chopped spinach
2 cups shredded
 mozzarella cheese
2 1/2 tablespoons grated
 Parmesan cheese
1 egg
1/4 cup melted butter
1/8 teaspoon each sage,
 thyme and pepper
1/4 cup melted butter

- Remove and chop mushroom stems. Remove casings from sausage. Sauté chopped stems and sausage with onion and garlic in olive oil in skillet.
- Blanch thawed spinach for 2 to 3 minutes; immerse in ice water. Press dry.
- Mix spinach with sausage mixture in bowl. Add cheeses, egg, 1/4 cup butter, sage, thyme and pepper; mix well.
- Spoon filling into mushroom caps. Arrange in baking dish. Bake at 375 degrees for 15 to 20 minutes or until golden brown. Drizzle with 1/4 cup butter.
- Yield: 20 servings.

Mushroom Pâté

1/3 cup chopped shallots
1/2 clove of garlic, minced
1/3 cup chopped fennel
    bulb
1/4 cup butter
2 eggs
3 ounces cream cheese,
    softened
4 cups finely chopped
    mushrooms
3/4 cup fine bread crumbs
1/2 tablespoon chopped
    fresh basil
1/4 teaspoon oregano
Salt and pepper to taste
1 egg yolk, at room
    temperature
1 teaspoon Dijon mustard
2 teaspoons lemon juice
1 teaspoon sage
1 tablespoon chopped
    fresh fennel leaves
1 cup oil

- Line buttered loaf pan with waxed paper, leaving 1 1/2-inch overhang.
- Sauté shallots, garlic and fennel bulb in butter in saucepan for 5 minutes.
- Beat eggs in mixer bowl. Add cream cheese; mix well. Stir in mushrooms, bread crumbs, sautéed vegetables, basil, oregano, salt and pepper. Spoon into prepared loaf pan. Bake at 400 degrees for 1 1/2 hours or until tester comes out clean. Cool to room temperature.
- Place egg yolk in warm bowl. Add mustard, lemon juice, sage, fennel leaves, salt and pepper; mix well. Whisk in oil drop by drop until mixture begins to emulsify. Add remaining oil in thin stream, whisking constantly until thickened. Serve with paté.
- May poach egg slightly to reduce danger of salmonella.
- Yield: 8 servings.

Seafood-Stuffed Mushrooms

12 large stuffing
    mushrooms
1 medium onion, chopped
1/2 cup margarine or butter
1/2 cup white wine
Bread crumbs
2 cans tiny shrimp,
    drained
1 can crab meat, drained
1 cup shredded Cheddar
    cheese

- Remove and chop mushroom stems.
- Sauté onion in margarine in skillet until tender. Add mushroom stems. Sauté for 1 minute; remove from heat.
- Stir in wine and enough bread crumbs to make of oatmeal consistency. Add shrimp, crab meat and cheese in bowl; mix well.
- Spoon into mushroom caps; arrange on baking sheet. Bake, covered, at 350 degrees for 20 minutes. Bake, uncovered, for 20 minutes longer.
- Yield: 12 servings.

Onion and Cheese Puffs

1 cup water
1/3 cup butter
1 cup flour
1/4 teaspoon garlic powder
1 teaspoon salt
4 eggs
3/4 cup shredded Swiss
   cheese
1 small Bermuda onion,
   chopped

- Bring water and butter to a rolling boil in saucepan. Stir in flour, garlic powder and salt. Cook over low heat for 1 minute or until mixture forms ball, stirring constantly. Remove from heat.
- Beat in eggs until smooth. Stir in cheese and onion.
- Drop by scant teaspoonfuls 1 inch apart onto lightly greased baking sheet. Bake at 400 degrees for 20 to 25 minutes or until puffed and brown. Serve warm.
- May press a pimento-stuffed olive, a small cube of ham and/or cheese or a peanut into each puff, covering completely, before baking.
- Yield: 72 servings.

Open-Faced Reubens

14 slices dark rye bread,
   toasted
Prepared mustard
1 (16-ounce) can
   sauerkraut, drained
2 (3-ounce) packages
   corned beef, finely
   chopped
2 cups shredded Swiss
   cheese
1/2 cup mayonnaise
1/2 teaspoon horseradish
   sauce

- Spread toasted bread lightly with mustard; place on ungreased baking sheet.
- Chop sauerkraut with scissors. Combine with corned beef, cheese, mayonnaise and horseradish sauce in bowl; mix well.
- Spread 1/3 cup corned beef mixture on each slice of toast. Bake at 375 degrees for 10 minutes or until cheese melts. Cut each slice into halves.
- May substitute ham for corned beef.
- Yield: 28 servings.

Taco Tartlets

1 pound ground beef
2 tablespoons taco
  seasoning mix
2 tablespoons ice water
1 cup sour cream
3 tablespoons red taco
  sauce
2 ounces black olives,
  chopped
1 cup coarsely crushed
  tortilla chips
1/2 cup shredded Cheddar
  cheese

- Combine ground beef with taco seasoning mix and water in bowl; mix well. Press mixture over bottom and sides of miniature muffin cups to form shells.
- Combine sour cream, taco sauce, olives and 3/4 cup tortilla chips in bowl; mix well. Spoon into prepared cups, mounding slightly. Top with remaining 1/4 cup tortilla chips and cheese.
- Bake at 375 degrees for 10 minutes or until ground beef is cooked through. Serve with additional taco sauce.
- Yield: 36 servings.

Baked Clams Italiano

1 (10-ounce) can minced
  clams
1 tablespoon grated onion
1 tablespoon minced
  parsley
1/8 teaspoon oregano
1/4 cup bread crumbs
2 tablespoons olive oil
1 teaspoon garlic salt
2 tablespoons bread
  crumbs
2 tablespoons grated
  Parmesan cheese

- Drain clams, reserving 3 tablespoons broth.
- Sauté onion, parsley, oregano and 1/4 cup bread crumbs in heated olive oil in skillet for 2 minutes or until onion is golden brown; remove from heat. Stir in clams, reserved broth and garlic salt.
- Spoon into 12 clam shells or shell dishes. Sprinkle with mixture of 2 tablespoons bread crumbs and cheese. Place on baking sheet.
- Bake at 375 degrees for 25 minutes or until top is golden brown and crusty.
- Yield: 6 servings.

Bayou Seafood Hors D'Oeuvres

1/4 cup instant minced
  onions
1/4 cup water
2 (6-ounce) cans crab
  meat or tuna, drained,
  flaked
2 eggs, slightly beaten
1/2 cup dry bread crumbs
2 tablespoons parsley
  flakes
1 1/2 teaspoons dry
  mustard
Ground red pepper to
  taste
1/4 teaspoon black pepper
Oil for frying

- Soak instant onion in water in bowl for 10 minutes. Add crab meat, eggs, bread crumbs, parsley, mustard, red pepper and black pepper; mix well. Shape into 1-inch balls.
- Heat 2 inches hot oil to 375 degrees in heavy saucepan. Fry balls a few at a time for 1 minute or until golden brown; remove with slotted spoon to drain.
- Serve with cucumber slices. May keep warm in single layer in shallow baking pan in 250-degree oven for up to 30 minutes.
- Yield: 12 to 16 servings.

Foo Yung Fritters

6 eggs
1 cup flour
1 1/2 teaspoons baking
  powder
1 tablespoon soy sauce
1/2 teaspoon
  Worcestershire sauce
1/2 teaspoon salt
1 can bean sprouts, drained
1 envelope onion soup mix
1 can mushroom stems
  and pieces, drained
1 (6-ounce) can shrimp,
  drained, chopped

- Beat eggs slightly in large mixer bowl. Blend in flour, baking powder, soy sauce, Worcestershire sauce and salt. Stir in bean sprouts, soup mix, mushrooms and shrimp.
- Drop by teaspoonfuls into 1/2 inch hot oil in skillet. Fry for 2 or 3 minutes on each side or until golden brown; drain.
- May freeze and reheat on rack in shallow baking pan in 350-degree oven for 10 to 12 minutes.
- Yield: 8 servings.

Shrimp Mini Pizzas

2 envelopes dry yeast
2 cups warm water
1/4 cup oil
2 teaspoons sugar
2 teaspoons salt
4 1/2 to 5 1/4 cups flour
1 (15-ounce) can tomato
  sauce
1 1/2 teaspoons Italian
  seasoning
3 (4-ounce) cans small
  shrimp, drained
1 medium onion, chopped
3/4 cup sliced black olives
1/2 large green bell
  pepper, chopped
1 1/2 cups shredded
  mozzarella cheese
2/3 cup grated Parmesan
  cheese

- Dissolve yeast in warm water in bowl. Add oil, sugar, salt and 4 cups flour; beat until smooth. Knead in enough remaining flour to make an easily handled dough. Knead for 3 to 5 minutes or until smooth and elastic.

- Place in greased bowl, turning to coat surface. Let rise, covered, in warm place for 45 minutes or until doubled in bulk. Punch dough down.

- Roll into two 12x16-inch rectangles on lightly floured surface. Cut each into twelve 4-inch circles. Place on ungreased baking sheet, shaping rims.

- Mix tomato sauce and Italian seasoning. Spoon 1 tablespoon mixture onto each circle. Top with remaining ingredients.

- Bake at 400 degrees for 15 minutes.

- Yield: 24 servings.

Rolled Shrimp Canapés

10 slices bacon
1 pound fresh or frozen
  medium shrimp,
  peeled, deveined
1 1/2 ounces cream cheese
  with chives, softened
2 teaspoons lemon juice
Hot pepper sauce to taste

- Cut bacon slices into halves crosswise. Cook in skillet for 4 minutes or until partially cooked; drain.

- Split shrimp into halves lengthwise. Spread 1 cut side with 1/2 teaspoon cream cheese; replace cut sides together. Brush with mixture of lemon juice and pepper sauce. Wrap with bacon slices; secure with wooden picks.

- Place on rack in broiler pan. Broil 4 to 5 inches from heat source for 2 to 3 minutes. Turn shrimp. Broil for 2 minutes longer or until shrimp are cooked through. Serve hot.

- Yield: 16 to 20 servings.

The Balsams Hot Buttered Rum

1/4 cup butter, softened
2 cup packed dark brown
　sugar
1 teaspoon cinnamon
1/4 teaspoon nutmeg
1/2 teaspoon ground cloves
Rum

- Combine butter, brown sugar, cinnamon nutmeg and cloves in bowl; mix until smooth. Spoon into covered jar. Chill until needed.
- Combine 1 heaping teaspoon brown sugar mixture with 1 cup boiling water and 1 1/2 ounces rum in mug for each serving; mix well. Garnish with orange slices.
- Yield: 100 servings.

Banana Supershake

2 ripe bananas, chopped
1/3 cup lemon juice
1 (14-ounce) can
　sweetened condensed
　milk
1 cup cold water
2 cups ice cubes

- Combine bananas, lemon juice, condensed milk and water in blender container; process until smooth.
- Add ice gradually, process until of desired consistency. May store in refrigerator.
- Reduce bananas to 1/2 cup and add 1 1/2 cups fresh strawberries or 1 cup frozen unsweetened strawberries for Strawberry-Banana Supershake.
- Yield: 5 servings.

Pink Elephant Punch

2 quarts cranberry juice
　cocktail
2 cups pineapple juice
1 fifth of vodka
1 quart ginger ale
Ice

- Combine cranberry juice, pineapple juice and vodka in punch bowl; mix well.
- Add ginger ale and ice just before serving. Ladle into punch cups.
- Yield: 48 servings.

Sunday Brunch Bloody Marys

1 large can vegetable juice
  cocktail
2 cups orange juice
¹/2 cup lemon juice
2 to 3 cups vodka
2 tablespoons
  Worcestershire sauce
1 teaspoon hot pepper
  sauce
1 teaspoon (or more)
  celery salt

- Combine vegetable juice cocktail, orange juice, lemon juice, vodka, Worcestershire sauce, pepper sauce and celery salt in pitcher; mix well.
- Pour over ice in glasses. Garnish with sliced lime and celery sticks.
- Yield: 20 servings.

Raspberry Blossom

Seltzer water
Ice
³/4 ounce vodka
³/4 ounce black raspberry
  liqueur

- Fill glass with seltzer water and ice. Stir in vodka and liqueur gently.
- Yield: 1 serving.

Café Godiva

2 ounces Godiva liqueur
6 ounces hot black coffee
Whipped cream (optional)

- Stir liqueur into coffee in cup. Top with whipped cream.
- Yield: 1 serving.

Make ice cubes of tea or fruit juice, so melting ice enhances the
flavor of your summer beverage rather than weakens it.

SOUPS

THE GREEN • WATERBURY

Easter
Seals

Avocado Soup

1 (6-ounce) can
  mushroom stems and
  pieces
2 tablespoons butter
2 tablespoons minced
  onion
2 tablespoons cornstarch
3 cups chicken broth
Salt and pepper to taste
1 large avocado, chopped

- Drain mushrooms, reserving liquid. Chop mushrooms.
- Melt butter in saucepan. Stir in onion. Cook until tender, stirring constantly. Add mushrooms; mix well. Cook for 1 to 2 minutes or until tender.
- Combine cornstarch with 1/2 cup broth in bowl; mix well. Add remaining broth; mix well. Stir into mushroom mixture. Add reserved liquid; mix well.
- Cook until thickened, stirring constantly. Season with salt and pepper.
- Stir in avocado just before serving. Cook just until heated through, stirring constantly.
- Ladle into soup bowls.
- May prepare soup base, chill and reheat, adding avocado just before serving.
- Yield: 6 servings.

Broccoli Cheese Soup

3/4 bunch broccoli
2 cups chicken stock
1 1/2 cups shredded carrots
1 stalk celery, finely
  chopped
1/3 cup clarified butter
1/3 cup flour
3 cups warm milk
1 onion, finely chopped
2/3 cup shredded sharp
  Cheddar cheese
2 teaspoons salt
1/2 teaspoon pepper
1 teaspoon chicken
  bouillon granules

- Shred broccoli stalks, reserving flowerets for another use.
- Bring shredded broccoli, stock, carrots and celery to a simmer in stockpot.
- Combine butter and flour in saucepan; mix well. Stir in milk and onion. Cook until consistency of thin gravy, stirring constantly. Stir in cheese. Cook until cheese melts, stirring constantly.
- Stir into broccoli mixture. Add salt, pepper and chicken bouillon.
- Ladle into soup bowls.
- Yield: 6 to 8 servings.

Carrot Bisque

3 to 5 slices bacon,
  chopped
1¼ pounds carrots,
  coarsely chopped
5 ounces mushrooms,
  coarsely chopped
½ cup coarsely chopped
  scallions with tops
1 cup chopped celery with
  leaves
5½ cups chicken stock
1 teaspoon chopped fresh
  thyme
1 small bay leaf
1¼ cups half and half
Salt and pepper to taste

- Fry bacon in saucepan until crisp, stirring constantly. Add carrots, mushrooms, scallions and celery, stirring until vegetables are coated with bacon drippings.
- Sauté vegetables for 5 minutes or until scallions are tender; reduce heat.
- Simmer, covered, for 10 minutes. Stir in chicken stock, thyme and bay leaf. Bring to a boil; reduce heat.
- Simmer, covered, for 50 minutes. Cool slightly. Discard bay leaf.
- Process in 2 batches in blender or food processor until puréed. Return mixture to saucepan. Stir in half and half.
- Cook over medium heat just until heated through, stirring frequently; do not boil. Remove from heat; season with salt and pepper.
- Ladle into soup bowls. Garnish with scallion tops.
- Yield: 6 to 8 servings.

Chili

2 pounds ground beef
1 large onion, chopped
3 or 4 cloves of garlic,
  finely chopped
Oil for sautéing
2 (35-ounce) cans Italian
  tomatoes, chopped
2 (16-ounce) jars chunky
  hot salsa
1 tablespoon chili powder
2 (19-ounce) cans red
  kidney beans, drained

- Brown ground beef with onion and garlic in oil in saucepan, stirring until ground beef is crumbly; drain.
- Stir in tomatoes. Add salsa and chili powder; mix well.
- Simmer for 30 minutes, stirring occasionally. Stir in kidney beans.
- Simmer for 20 minutes, stirring occasionally; do not boil.
- Ladle into soup bowls. Garnish with sour cream or shredded cheese.
- Yield: 10 to 12 servings.

Meatball Soup

1 1/2 pounds ground beef
1 egg, slightly beaten
1/2 cup dry bread crumbs
1 medium potato, finely
    chopped
1 small onion, finely
    chopped
1/4 cup milk
1 teaspoon salt
1 tablespoon snipped
    fresh parsley
1 tablespoon oil
1 (28-ounce) can whole
    tomatoes, chopped
1 (10-ounce) can beef
    broth
2 cups water
2 medium carrots, sliced
2 medium potatoes, cut
    into 1/2-inch slices
1 small stalk celery,
    chopped
1/4 cup chopped snipped
    parsley
1 envelope onion soup mix
1 bay leaf
1/2 teaspoon basil
1/4 teaspoon pepper

- Combine ground beef, egg, bread crumbs, 1 potato, onion, milk, salt and 1 tablespoon parsley in bowl; mix well. Shape into 1 1/2-inch balls.
- Sauté meatballs in oil in heavy saucepan until light brown. Remove meatballs to platter, discarding pan drippings.
- Bring undrained tomatoes, broth, water, carrots, 2 potatoes, celery, 1/4 cup parsley, soup mix, bay leaf, basil and pepper to a boil in same saucepan; reduce heat.
- Simmer, covered, for 30 minutes, stirring occasionally. Add meatballs; mix well.
- Simmer, covered, for 20 minutes, stirring occasionally. Discard bay leaf.
- Ladle into soup bowls.
- Yield: 8 servings.

Add interest to your soups with a different garnish.
Try shredded cheese, grated hard-boiled egg,
lemon slices, sunflower or sesame seeds, a dollop of sour
cream or yogurt, alfalfa sprouts or roasted nuts.

Hearty Beef Soup

2 pounds extra-lean round
   steak, cut into
   bite-sized pieces
1½ cups sliced carrots
2 bay leaves
2 medium onions, chopped
1 cup chopped celery
3 cups vegetable juice
   cocktail
2 to 3 tablespoons
   Worcestershire sauce
6 cups water
3 (10-ounce) cans beef
   broth
Salt and pepper to taste
2 cups cooked rice

- Brown beef in stockpot; drain.
- Add carrots, bay leaves, onions, celery, vegetable juice cocktail, Worcestershire sauce, water, broth, salt and pepper; mix well.
- Bring mixture to a boil; reduce heat. Simmer for 2½ to 3 hours or until of desired consistency. Discard bay leaves.
- Stir in rice just before serving. Ladle into soup bowls.
- Yield: 8 to 10 servings.

Chicken and Corn Soup

4 cups chicken broth
1 small onion, chopped
1 stalk celery, chopped
2 hard-boiled eggs,
   chopped
1 (10-ounce) package
   frozen corn
1 cup chopped cooked
   chicken
1 cup cooked narrow
   noodles
2 tablespoons chopped
   fresh parsley
Salt and pepper to taste

- Combine broth, onion, celery, eggs, corn, chicken, noodles, parsley, salt and pepper in large saucepan; mix well.
- Simmer for 1 hour, stirring occasionally.
- Ladle into soup bowls.
- May add 1 can chopped stewed tomatoes.
- Yield: 6 to 8 servings.

Creamy Clam Chowder

1 medium onion, finely
   chopped
3 tablespoons butter
2 tablespoons flour
1/2 to 1 cup clam juice
1 cup milk
2 cups light cream
2 (8-ounce) cans minced
   clams, drained
2 tablespoons Madeira
1/2 teaspoon thyme
1 teaspoon salt
Cayenne pepper to taste
Freshly ground black
   pepper to taste
2 tablespoons chopped
   fresh parsley

- Sauté onion in 1 tablespoon butter in skillet until tender. Stir in 2 tablespoons butter and flour. Cook for 1 minute, stirring constantly. Stir in clam juice, milk and cream.
- Cook over medium heat until thickened, stirring constantly. Remove from heat.
- Stir in clams, Madeira, thyme, salt, cayenne pepper and black pepper. Chill, covered, to enhance flavor.
- Reheat. Ladle into soup bowls. Sprinkle with parsley.
- May add 1 beaten egg to soup to thicken. May substitute 24 raw clams for canned clams.
- Yield: 6 servings.

Manhattan Clam Chowder

2 (6-ounce) cans whole
   clams
1 (6-ounce) can minced
   clams
6 slices bacon, chopped
2 cups water
2 (8-ounce) cans tomato
   sauce
2 medium onions, chopped
4 carrots, chopped
4 potatoes, chopped
2 stalks celery, chopped
1 teaspoon salt
1/2 teaspoon white pepper
1 teaspoon thyme
1 bay leaf

- Drain clams, reserving liquid. Combine reserved liquid with enough water to measure 4 cups.
- Fry bacon in stockpot until crisp. Stir in mixture of water and tomato sauce. Add onions, carrots, potatoes, celery, salt, white pepper, thyme and bay leaf; mix well.
- Simmer for 20 minutes, stirring occasionally. Add clam liquid mixture; mix well.
- Simmer until vegetables are tender, stirring occasionally. Stir in clams. Discard bay leaf.
- Ladle into soup bowls.
- Yield: 6 to 8 servings.

J. B.'s New England Clam Chowder

3 dozen cherrystone or
  littleneck clams
1 small onion
Parsley sprigs to taste
2 cups finely chopped
  onions
1 cup chopped celery
$1/4$ cup butter
2 cups clam broth
$1^1/2$ teaspoons thyme
$1^1/2$ teaspoons oregano
$1^1/2$ teaspoons pepper
$1/2$ cup chopped fresh
  parsley
2 medium potatoes,
  chopped
4 cups whipping cream

- Scrub clams. Add enough water to 2-quart saucepan to measure 1 inch. Add clams, 1 onion and parsley sprigs.
- Cook, covered, until clams open. Remove clams to platter with slotted spoon; reserve liquid and discard onion and parsley. Shell clams. Chill for 10 minutes. Chop clams.
- Sauté chopped onions and celery in butter in stockpot until tender. Add clam broth, seasonings, chopped parsley and potatoes.
- Cook, covered, for 30 minutes, stirring occasionally. Stir in reserved liquid, clams and whipping cream.
- Simmer just until heated through, stirring constantly; adjust seasonings.
- Ladle into soup bowls.
- Yield: 6 to 8 servings.

West Falmouth Clam Chowder

25 to 30 large quahaug
  clams
1 slice salt pork, cut into
  strips
1 large onion, chopped
Oil
5 or 6 potatoes, chopped
Pepper to taste

- Rinse clams. Remove clams from shells, reserving liquid; chop clams. Combine reserved juice with equal amount of water; mix well.
- Sauté salt pork and onion in oil in stockpot until onion is tender but not brown. Stir in clam juice mixture and potatoes.
- Simmer until potatoes are tender, stirring occasionally. Stir in clams.
- Simmer for 10 minutes, stirring occasionally. Season with pepper.
- Ladle into soup bowls.
- May add milk to soup bowls if desired.
- Yield: 16 servings.

Fish Chowder

2 pounds frozen halibut
  or haddock fillets,
  thawed
3 cups water
4 medium potatoes, cut
  into 1/2-inch pieces
1 large onion, chopped
1 medium green bell
  pepper, chopped
1 medium tomato, peeled,
  chopped
1 cup half and half
1 3/4 teaspoons salt
1/4 teaspoon pepper
1/4 teaspoon tarragon
1/3 cup shredded Cheddar
  cheese

- Bring fillets and water to a boil in large saucepan; reduce heat. Simmer, covered, for 10 to 15 minutes or until fish flakes easily. Transfer fish to platter, reserving broth. Cut fish into bite-sized pieces.
- Combine 1 cup reserved broth, potatoes, onion and green pepper in saucepan. Cook for 15 minutes or until potatoes are tender. Stir in remaining reserved broth, fish, tomato, half and half, salt, pepper and tarragon.
- Cook just until heated through, stirring constantly.
- Ladle into soup bowls; sprinkle with cheese.
- Yield: 8 servings.

Cucumber Soup

1 cucumber, peeled,
  chopped
1 cucumber, chopped
2 cups sour cream
1/2 medium onion,
  chopped
1 (10-ounce) can chicken
  broth
Parsley sprigs
Salt and pepper to taste
Nutmeg to taste

- Combine cucumbers, sour cream, onion, broth, parsley, salt, pepper and nutmeg in blender container.
- Process until blended. Chill, covered, in refrigerator.
- Pour into soup bowls.
- Yield: 6 to 8 servings.

Chop unused broccoli and asparagus stems in the food processor
and store them in a plastic bag in the freezer for use in soups.

Lentil and Barley Soup

3/4 cup lentils
3/4 cup chopped onion
3/4 cup chopped celery
1 clove of garlic, minced
1/4 cup margarine or butter
6 cups water
1 (28-ounce) can
 tomatoes, chopped
3/4 cup pearl barley
6 vegetarian bouillon
 cubes
1/2 teaspoon rosemary,
 crushed
1/2 teaspoon oregano,
 crushed
1/4 teaspoon pepper
1 cup thinly sliced carrots
1 cup shredded Swiss
 cheese

- Sort lentils; rinse.
- Sauté onion, celery and garlic in margarine in stockpot until tender. Add lentils, water, undrained tomatoes, barley, bouillon, rosemary, oregano and pepper; mix well. Bring to a boil; reduce heat.
- Simmer, covered, for 45 minutes, stirring occasionally. Stir in carrots.
- Simmer, covered, for 15 minutes or until carrots are tender-crisp, stirring occasionally.
- Ladle into soup bowls; sprinkle with cheese.
- Yield: 5 servings.

Mushroom and Barley Soup

1/2 cup barley
1 1/2 cups water
1 medium onion, chopped
2 tablespoons butter
2 medium cloves of garlic,
 minced
1 pound mushrooms,
 sliced
1/2 teaspoon salt
5 tablespoons soy sauce
5 tablespoons sherry
4 1/2 cups water
Ground pepper to taste

- Bring barley and 1 1/2 cups water to a boil in saucepan; reduce heat. Simmer, covered, for 30 minutes or until barley is tender.
- Sauté onion in butter in saucepan over medium heat for 5 minutes. Stir in garlic, mushrooms and salt.
- Cook, covered, for 12 minutes. Add soy sauce and sherry; mix well. Stir into barley. Add 4 1/2 cups water and pepper; mix well. Cook for 20 minutes longer, stirring occasionally.
- Ladle into soup bowls.
- Yield: 6 servings.

Mushroom and Crab Meat Soup

8 ounces mushrooms,
 sliced
¹/4 cup butter
2 teaspoons grated onion
2 tomatoes, sliced
2 (6-ounce) cans crab meat
¹/2 teaspoon salt
Cayenne pepper to taste
1 cup cream
2 teaspoons minced
 parsley
1 teaspoon minced chives
¹/4 cup sherry

- Sauté mushrooms in butter in saucepan for 5 minutes. Stir in onion and tomatoes.
- Cook for 5 minutes, stirring frequently. Add crab meat, salt and cayenne pepper.
- Cook for 1 minute, stirring constantly. Stir in cream.
- Bring to a boil. Remove from heat. Stir in parsley, chives and sherry.
- Ladle into soup bowls.
- Yield: 4 servings.

Pimento Cream Soup

4 ounces spaghetti
1 cup minced celery
4 cups boiling chicken or
 beef broth
1 tablespoon minced onion
2 (4-ounce) jars pimentos,
 finely chopped
2 egg yolks
¹/2 cup cream
Salt and pepper to taste

- Combine spaghetti and celery with boiling chicken broth in saucepan; mix well.
- Simmer, covered, for 20 minutes. Stir in onion and pimentos.
- Beat egg yolks and cream in mixer bowl until blended. Stir a small amount of hot broth mixture into egg yolk mixture; stir egg yolk mixture into hot broth. Season with salt and pepper.
- Ladle into soup bowls.
- Yield: 4 to 6 servings.

Make a quick soup by adding a rounded tablespoon of shredded crab meat for each serving to hot chicken broth and seasoning lightly with soy sauce or dry sherry and chopped green onions.

Potato and Leek Soup

4 or 5 leeks
1/4 cup margarine
4 cups half and half
6 chicken bouillon cubes
Salt and pepper to taste
1 gallon water
8 to 10 medium potatoes, chopped

- Trim leeks to within 1 inch of bulb; cut into thin slices.
- Sauté leeks in margarine in stockpot until tender but not brown. Stir in half and half, bouillon cubes, salt, pepper, water and potatoes.
- Cook until potatoes are tender, stirring occasionally. Remove 1/2 of the potatoes; mash. Return mashed potatoes to stockpot; mix well. Cook just until heated through, stirring constantly.
- Ladle into soup bowls.
- Yield: 14 to 16 servings.

Swiss Potato Soup

1 chicken bouillon cube
1 cup boiling water
3 cups chopped potatoes
1/2 cup chopped celery
1/4 cup chopped onion
1 teaspoon parsley flakes
1 teaspoon salt
Pepper to taste
2 to 4 tablespoons flour
2 1/2 cups milk
6 ounces Swiss cheese, shredded
6 slices crisp-fried bacon, crumbled

- Combine bouillon cube and boiling water in saucepan, stirring until bouillon dissolves. Add potatoes, celery, onion, parsley flakes, salt and pepper; mix well.
- Simmer, covered, for 10 minutes, stirring occasionally.
- Combine flour with enough milk to moisten in bowl; mix well. Stir into vegetable mixture. Add remaining milk; mix well.
- Cook until thickened, stirring constantly. Stir in cheese and bacon. Cook until cheese melts, stirring constantly.
- Ladle into soup bowls.
- Yield: 6 to 8 servings.

Pumpkin Soup

1 large onion, chopped
1 medium leek bulb, chopped
1/4 cup butter
2 cups fresh or canned pumpkin
4 cups low-sodium chicken broth
1/2 teaspoon curry powder
1/4 teaspoon nutmeg
1/4 teaspoon ginger
1 bay leaf
1 cup half and half
Salt to taste

- Sauté onion and leek in butter in large saucepan until tender. Stir in pumpkin, chicken broth, curry powder, nutmeg, ginger and bay leaf. Bring to a boil; reduce heat.
- Simmer for 15 minutes, stirring occasionally. Discard bay leaf. Process in blender until puréed. Return to saucepan. Stir in half and half.
- Simmer just until heated through, stirring constantly. Season with salt.
- Ladle into soup bowls.
- Yield: 6 servings.

Cream of Spinach Soup

1/4 cup chopped onion
1/4 cup chopped celery
6 tablespoons butter
1/3 cup flour
1 (8-ounce) can whole kernel corn, drained
1 (10-ounce) package frozen chopped spinach, thawed, drained
4 1/2 cups milk
1 tablespoon chicken bouillon granules
1 teaspoon salt
1/2 teaspoon parsley flakes
1/2 teaspoon thyme
1 bay leaf, crushed
1/8 teaspoon pepper
1 teaspoon prepared mustard
1/4 teaspoon hot pepper sauce
4 tablespoons butter, cut into 4 pieces

- Sauté onion and celery in 6 tablespoons butter in 3-quart saucepan for 3 to 4 minutes or until vegetables are tender-crisp. Remove from heat.
- Stir in flour. Add corn, spinach, milk, bouillon, salt, parsley flakes, thyme, bay leaf, pepper, mustard and hot pepper sauce; mix well.
- Cook over medium-low heat for 20 to 25 minutes or until thickened, stirring occasionally.
- Ladle into soup bowls; top each with a tablespoon of butter.
- Yield: 4 servings.

Acorn Squash Soup

2 medium acorn squash,
  cut into halves, seeded
4 cups water
1 large onion, sliced
1 yellow bell pepper,
  sliced
3 tablespoons butter
3 apples, chopped
1 tablespoon
  Worcestershire sauce
Salt and pepper to taste
3 cups chicken broth
1 teaspoon curry powder
2 cups half and half

- Bring squash and water to a boil in saucepan. Boil for 15 to 20 minutes or until tender. Drain, reserving liquid. Cool. Scoop squash pulp into bowl, discarding skin.
- Sauté onion and yellow pepper in butter in large saucepan until onion is tender. Add squash pulp, reserved liquid, apples, Worcestershire sauce, salt, pepper, chicken broth and curry powder; mix well. Bring to a boil; reduce heat. Simmer for 15 minutes, stirring occasionally.
- Purée squash mixture in blender or food processor. Return to saucepan. Stir in half and half; adjust seasonings.
- Cook over medium heat just until heated through, stirring frequently; do not boil.
- Ladle into soup bowls.
- Yield: 8 to 10 servings.

Fresh Tomato Soup

1 medium onion, chopped
1 clove of garlic, minced
1 tablespoon oil
4 cups chopped peeled
  tomatoes
1 cup chicken broth
1 tablespoon chopped
  fresh parsley
1/2 teaspoon salt
1/8 teaspoon pepper
1/3 cup grated Parmesan
  cheese

- Sauté onion and garlic in oil in saucepan over medium heat for 4 minutes or until onion is tender. Stir in tomatoes, broth, parsley, salt and pepper. Bring to a boil; reduce heat. Simmer, covered, for 15 minutes, stirring occasionally.
- Process tomato mixture in blender until puréed. Return to saucepan.
- Cook just until heated through, stirring constantly.
- Ladle into soup bowls; sprinkle with cheese.
- Yield: 6 servings.

Cold Zucchini Soup

3 or 4 zucchini, sliced
2 medium onions, cut into
  quarters
2 tablespoons (about)
  Italian seasoning
Salt and pepper to taste

- Bring zucchini, onions, Italian seasoning, salt, pepper and enough water to cover to a boil in saucepan; reduce heat.
- Simmer for 7 minutes or until vegetables are tender, stirring occasionally; drain.
- Process zucchini mixture in food processor until mashed. Process in blender until puréed.
- Chill, covered, for 8 to 12 hours.
- Ladle into soup bowls; garnish with dollop of sour cream.
- Yield: 6 servings.

Zucchini and Sausage Soup

1 pound Italian sweet or
  hot sausage, crumbled
2 cups 1/2-inch slices
  celery
2 or 3 zucchini, sliced
1 cup chopped onion
2 (28-ounce) cans
  tomatoes
2 teaspoons salt
1 teaspoon Italian
  seasoning
1 teaspoon oregano
1 teaspoon sugar
1/2 teaspoon basil
1/4 teaspoon garlic powder
1 cup red wine
1/2 cup water
2 green bell peppers, cut
  into 1/2-inch pieces
Grated Parmesan cheese
  to taste

- Brown sausage in stockpot, stirring until crumbly; drain. Add celery; mix well.
- Cook for 10 minutes, stirring occasionally. Stir in zucchini, onion, tomatoes, salt, Italian seasoning, oregano, sugar, basil, garlic powder, red wine and water.
- Simmer, covered, for 20 minutes, stirring occasionally. Add green peppers; mix well.
- Cook, covered, for 10 minutes, stirring occasionally.
- Ladle into soup bowls; sprinkle with cheese.
- Yield: 12 servings.

SALADS

CONGREGATIONAL CHURCH • GUILFORD

Stuffed Apple Salad

4 stalks celery hearts,
  finely chopped
6 red delicious apples
2 tablespoons lemon juice
1 cup whipping cream
4 teaspoons lemon juice
2 tablespoons raw sugar
1/2 clove of garlic, finely
  chopped
1 teaspoon white pepper
1/8 teaspoon salt
1/2 cup golden raisins
2 tablespoons pine nuts
1/2 cup chopped walnuts

- Combine celery with ice water in bowl. Let stand until crisp. Drain; pat dry.
- Wipe apples with damp cloth to polish. Cut 1/2 inch slice off top. Scoop out pulp and seeds carefully, leaving shell. Discard seeds. Chop pulp finely. Combine pulp and 2 tablespoons lemon juice in bowl; mix well. Stir in celery.
- Beat whipping cream in mixer bowl until soft peaks form. Fold in 4 teaspoons lemon juice, sugar, garlic, white pepper, salt, raisins, pine nuts and walnuts.
- Pour whipped cream mixture over apple mixture, tossing to coat. Spoon into apple shells. Garnish with walnut halves or well drained whole maraschino cherries with stems. Serve with small wedges of cheese on bed of watercress or lettuce.
- Yield: 6 servings.

Cheesy Fruit Mold

1 (6-ounce) package
  orange gelatin
1/2 cup sugar
2 1/2 cups boiling water
8 ounces cream cheese,
  softened
2 (13-ounce) cans crushed
  pineapple
2 cups shredded Cheddar
  cheese
2 cups cottage cheese
2 teaspoons lemon juice
2 cups plain yogurt
1/2 cup honey
Nutmeg to taste

- Dissolve gelatin and sugar in boiling water in mixer bowl; mix well. Beat in cream cheese until smooth. Stir in undrained pineapple, Cheddar cheese, cottage cheese and lemon juice.
- Pour into 12-cup mold. Chill for 8 hours or until set.
- Invert onto lettuce-lined platter. Serve with mixture of yogurt, honey and nutmeg.
- May substitute lime gelatin for orange gelatin.
- Yield: 12 servings.

Fruit and Nut Tossed Salad

1 cup fresh torn spinach
6 cups fresh torn romaine
  lettuce
1 cup red or green grape
  halves
1/2 cup slivered almonds,
  toasted
1 (11-ounce) can
  mandarin oranges,
  chilled, drained
1/2 cup oil
1/4 cup vinegar
1/4 cup sugar
1/2 teaspoon salt
1 small avocado, sliced

- Combine spinach, romaine lettuce, grapes, almonds and mandarin oranges in salad bowl; mix well.
- Combine oil, vinegar, sugar and salt in jar with lid, shaking to mix.
- Toss spinach mixture with some of the dressing. Top with sliced avocado. Serve remaining dressing with salad.
- Yield: 6 to 8 servings.

Waldorf Supreme

2 unpeeled apples,
  chopped
2 stalks celery, chopped
1/4 cup chopped pecans
1/2 cup mayonnaise
1/4 cup plus 2 tablespoons
  pear preserves
1 tablespoon lemon juice

- Combine apples, celery and pecans in bowl; mix well.
- Add mixture of mayonnaise, pear preserves and lemon juice, tossing to coat.
- Yield: 4 to 6 servings.

For **Elegant Ambrosia**, combine an 8-ounce can each
of drained mandarin oranges and pineapple chunks, a cup of
seedless grapes, a 15-ounce can of drained Royal Anne
cherries, a cup of marshmallows and a cup of sour cream.
Chill, covered, for 24 hours.

Avocado Surprise

3 (6-ounce) cans crab
  meat, drained, flaked
²/₃ cup mayonnaise
¹/₄ cup chili sauce
1 tablespoon sweet pickle
  relish
3 large avocados, cut into
  halves
3 hard-boiled eggs, finely
  chopped
1 tablespoon finely
  chopped fresh dillweed

- Place crab meat in bowl.
- Combine mayonnaise, chili sauce and pickle relish in bowl; mix well. Add enough mayonnaise mixture to crab meat to moisten or until of desired consistency; mix well.
- Fill each avocado half with crab meat mixture; sprinkle with mixture of eggs and dillweed. Top with remaining mayonnaise mixture.
- Yield: 6 servings.

Crab Louis

3 cups cooked crab meat
1 head iceberg lettuce,
  torn into bite-sized
  pieces
1 (6-ounce) jar marinated
  artichoke hearts,
  drained
1 avocado, sliced
3 tomatoes, cut into
  eighths
1 lemon, cut into 6 wedges
6 hard-boiled eggs, cut
  into halves
¹/₂ cup whipping cream
1 cup mayonnaise

- Arrange crab meat on 6 lettuce-lined salad plates. Arrange artichoke hearts, avocado slices, tomato wedges, 1 lemon wedge and 2 egg halves on each plate.
- Beat whipping cream in mixer bowl until stiff peaks form. Fold in mayonnaise.
- Pour dressing over crab meat mixture. Serve immediately.
- Yield: 6 servings.

Serve chicken or seafood salad in avocado halves, tomato
cups, melon rings or pineapple boats.

Curried Chicken Salad

2 cups seedless green
  grapes
2 cups chopped cooked
  chicken, chilled
1/2 cup sour cream
1/2 cup mayonnaise
2 tablespoons minced
  onion
1 tablespoon lemon juice
1 teaspoon curry powder
1/4 teaspoon salt
3/4 cup cashews
3/4 cup chopped cashews

- Combine grapes and chicken in bowl; mix well.
- Combine sour cream, mayonnaise, onion, lemon juice, curry powder and salt in bowl; mix well. Spoon over chicken mixture, tossing to coat.
- Chill, covered, for several hours. Stir in 3/4 cup cashews.
- Spoon chicken salad onto lettuce-lined salad plates; sprinkle with 3/4 cup chopped cashews. Garnish with grape clusters.
- Yield: 6 servings.

Chicken Salad with Corn and Peppers

1 1/2 pounds boneless
  chicken breasts with
  skin
1/2 cup lime juice
1 tablespoon oregano
Salt and pepper to taste
Oil to taste
2 cups fresh cooked corn
1 large red bell pepper,
  chopped
3 scallions, thinly sliced
2 tablespoons lime juice
1 teaspoon oregano
1/2 teaspoon cumin
1 bunch arugula or Boston
  lettuce, separated into
  leaves

- Rinse chicken and pat dry. Place in bowl.
- Pour mixture of 1/2 cup lime juice, 1 tablespoon oregano, salt and pepper over chicken, tossing to coat.
- Chill, covered, for 30 to 60 minutes. Drain; pat dry. Brush chicken with oil. Sprinkle with salt and pepper.
- Place chicken on oiled grill rack. Grill 6 inches from hot coals for 6 to 7 minutes per side or just until tender. Transfer chicken to cutting board. Let stand for 10 minutes. Cut into thin slices lengthwise, reserving any accumulated juices on cutting board.
- Combine corn, red pepper, scallions, 2 tablespoons lime juice, 1 teaspoon oregano, cumin, oil to taste, salt and pepper in bowl; mix well. Stir in chicken and reserved juices. Spoon the chicken salad on arugula-lined salad plates.
- Yield: 4 servings.

Chicken and Tarragon Salad

3 pounds chicken breast
  filets
$1/2$ cup sour cream
$1/2$ cup mayonnaise
1 tablespoon tarragon
$1/3$ cup chopped celery
$1/2$ cup chopped walnuts
Salt and pepper to taste

- Rinse chicken and pat dry. Place in baking pan. Bake at 350 degrees for 25 to 35 minutes or until tender, basting occasionally. Cool. Chop into bite-sized pieces.
- Combine sour cream and mayonnaise in bowl; mix well. Stir in tarragon. Add chicken and celery; mix well. Stir in walnuts, salt and pepper. Chill, covered, in refrigerator.
- Spoon chicken mixture on lettuce-lined salad plates. Garnish with chopped fresh parsley or finely chopped scallions. May serve as a sandwich filling.
- May substitute yogurt for sour cream and almonds for walnuts.
- Yield: 4 to 6 servings.

Taco Salad

1 to $1^{1}/2$ pounds ground
  beef
1 head romaine lettuce,
  separated into leaves
2 or 3 tomatoes, chopped
3 or 4 green onions, finely
  sliced
8 ounces Cheddar cheese,
  shredded
1 avocado, sliced
$1/2$ teaspoon garlic salt
$1/4$ teaspoon celery salt
1 (16-ounce) can kidney
  beans
5 tablespoons taco sauce
Mayonnaise to taste
Salt and pepper to taste
1 package tortilla chips

- Brown ground beef in skillet, stirring until crumbly; drain.
- Combine ground beef, romaine lettuce, tomatoes, green onions, cheese, avocado, garlic salt, celery salt and kidney beans in large salad bowl; mix well.
- Combine taco sauce, mayonnaise, salt and pepper in small bowl; mix well. Add to ground beef mixture with chips just before serving, tossing to coat.
- Yield: 12 servings.

Pasta and Broccoli Salad

2 cups broccoli flowerets
Salt to taste
8 ounces rotelle, cooked
  al dente, rinsed, drained
2 cups chopped tomatoes
1 (6-ounce) can oil-pack
  tuna
Pepper to taste
3 tablespoons red wine
  vinegar
1/2 cup olive oil
1/4 teaspoon red pepper
  flakes
1/2 cup finely chopped
  parsley
1/2 cup thinly sliced red
  onion
3/4 cup loosely packed
  fresh basil

- Combine broccoli and salt with enough water to cover in saucepan. Cook for 5 minutes or until tender-crisp; drain.
- Combine broccoli, pasta, tomatoes, tuna, pepper, wine vinegar, olive oil, red pepper flakes, parsley, red onion and basil in bowl; mix well.
- Serve at room temperature.
- May be prepared 1 day in advance and refrigerated overnight. Let stand until room temperature.
- Yield: 8 servings.

Pasta Salad

1 (16-ounce) package
  tricolor pasta, cooked,
  drained
1/2 jar Salad Supreme
  seasoning
1 bottle Italian salad
  dressing
1 tomato, chopped
1/2 large cucumber, sliced
1 cup broccoli flowerets
1/2 cup pitted black olives

- Combine pasta, Salad Supreme seasoning and salad dressing in bowl; mix well. Marinate, covered, in refrigerator overnight, turning occasionally.
- Stir in tomato, cucumber, broccoli and black olives.
- Marinate, covered, in refrigerator for 2 hours or longer.
- Yield: 6 to 8 servings.

Spinach Pasta Salad

8 ounces spinach noodles
4 ounces Genoa salami,
  julienned
1 medium green bell
  pepper, chopped
1 medium onion, chopped
1 bunch celery, chopped
16 to 20 canned artichoke
  hearts, cut into halves
1 tomato, cut into wedges
1/4 cup mayonnaise
1/4 cup sour cream
2 tablespoons tarragon
2 tablespoons vinegar
1 teaspoon chopped fresh
  basil
Salt and pepper to taste

- Cook noodles using package directions. Drain; rinse noodles. Chill, covered, in bowl in refrigerator.
- Combine salami, green pepper, onion and celery in large bowl; mix well. Stir in artichoke hearts and tomato. Add noodles, tossing to mix.
- Combine mayonnaise, sour cream, tarragon, vinegar, basil, salt and pepper in bowl; mix well. Add to noodle mixture, tossing to coat.
- Yield: 10 to 12 servings.

Avocado and Beet Salad

1 package unflavored
  gelatin
1/2 cup cold orange juice
1 (16-ounce) can sliced
  beets
2 tablespoons mayonnaise
3/4 teaspoon salt
1/4 teaspoon pepper
1/2 cup orange juice
4 avocados, cut into halves
Lettuce leaves
Juice of 1 lemon

- Combine gelatin and 1/2 cup orange juice in bowl; mix well. Let stand until softened.
- Drain beets, reserving liquid. Bring reserved beet liquid to a boil in saucepan. Add to gelatin mixture, stirring until gelatin dissolves.
- Combine gelatin mixture, beets, mayonnaise, salt, pepper and 1/2 cup orange juice in blender container. Process until smooth. Pour into bowl. Chill, covered, for 2 hours or until set.
- Arrange avocado halves on lettuce-lined serving platter; sprinkle with lemon juice. Place 1 scoop of beet mixture on each avocado half.
- Place bowl of mayonnaise in center of platter. Garnish with parsley sprigs.
- Yield: 8 servings.

Brussels Sprouts Salad

1 (10-ounce) package
  frozen Brussels sprouts
1 medium cucumber,
  sliced
1/4 cup wine vinegar
1/4 cup oil
1 teaspoon salt
1/2 teaspoon caraway seeds
1/4 teaspoon pepper
10 cherry tomatoes, cut
  into halves
4 lettuce cups

- Cook Brussels sprouts using package directions; drain. Place in bowl. Add cucumber; mix well.
- Combine wine vinegar, oil, salt, caraway seeds and pepper in covered container, shaking to mix. Pour over hot Brussels sprouts and cucumber, tossing to coat.
- Chill, covered, for 3 hours or longer. Stir in tomatoes.
- Spoon into lettuce cups on salad plates. Garnish with snipped parsley.
- Yield: 4 servings.

Tropical Cabbage Salad

1 cup flaked coconut
1 medium head cabbage,
  finely shredded
3/4 cup sour cream
2 1/2 tablespoons vinegar
3/4 teaspoon salt
1/4 teaspoon pepper
1 tablespoon sugar
Paprika to taste
Toasted coconut to taste

- Combine coconut and cabbage in salad bowl; mix well. Stir in mixture of sour cream, vinegar, salt, pepper and sugar. Sprinkle with paprika and toasted coconut.
- Toast coconut by spreading a thin layer of coconut on baking sheet. Bake at 350 degrees for 3 to 4 minutes or until light brown, stirring frequently.
- Yield: 6 to 8 servings.

Hot Cabbage Salad

2 cups finely sliced
  cabbage
2 tablespoons salt
2 tablespoons oil
2 tablespoons Italian
  salad dressing

- Combine cabbage and salt in bowl; mix well. Let stand for 30 minutes.
- Stir-fry cabbage in oil in skillet for 2 minutes. Remove cabbage to bowl. Add salad dressing, tossing to coat. Serve immediately.
- Yield: 4 servings.

Caesar Salad

1 clove of garlic, cut into halves
1 large head romaine lettuce, torn
8 anchovy fillets, chopped
1/3 cup olive oil
1 teaspoon Worcestershire sauce
1/2 teaspoon salt
1/4 teaspoon dry mustard
Freshly ground pepper to taste
1 lemon, cut into halves
1 cup garlic-flavored croutons
1/3 cup grated Parmesan cheese

- Rub large wooden salad bowl with garlic; discard 3/4 of the garlic. Place romaine in bowl.
- Combine anchovies, olive oil, Worcestershire sauce, salt, dry mustard and pepper in bowl; mix well. Pour over romaine, tossing to coat. Squeeze lemon over salad; mix well. Sprinkle with croutons and cheese; toss.
- Yield: 6 servings.

Eggless Caesar Salad

3 heads romaine lettuce, torn into bite-sized pieces
1 cup olive oil
1/2 cup fresh lemon juice
2 teaspoons minced garlic
1 teaspoon Worcestershire sauce
1 teaspoon Dijon mustard
White pepper to taste
1 small can anchovies, drained
1 cup grated Parmesan cheese
Croutons to taste

- Place romaine in large salad bowl.
- Process olive oil, lemon juice, garlic, Worcestershire sauce, Dijon mustard, white pepper, anchovies and cheese in blender until well blended. Pour over romaine, tossing to coat. Add croutons; toss.
- Serve on chilled salad plates with freshly ground pepper.
- Yield: 10 to 12 servings.

Corn and Black Bean Salad

2 (17-ounce) cans corn
   niblets, drained
2 (19-ounce) cans black
   beans, drained
1 large red bell pepper,
   chopped
6 stalks celery, chopped
5 or 6 scallions, chopped
2 tablespoons olive oil
$2/3$ cup balsamic vinegar
1 teaspoon Dijon mustard

- Combine corn, black beans, red pepper, celery and scallions in large bowl; mix well. Stir in mixture of olive oil, balsamic vinegar and Dijon mustard.
- Chill, covered, for 8 hours or longer, stirring occasionally.
- May add sliced carrots, mushrooms, crisp green beans or asparagus. May store in refrigerator for 2 to 3 days.
- Yield: 10 to 12 servings.

Grilled Eggplant Salad

2 small eggplants
Salt to taste
1 cup olive oil
3 tomatoes, sliced
1 cup shredded
   mozzarella cheese
$1/2$ cup calamata olives
2 tablespoons capers
Green olive oil to taste
Red wine vinegar to taste
Freshly ground pepper to
   taste
5 basil leaves, julienned

- Peel eggplant under running water; cut into 1-inch slices. Sprinkle with salt. Let stand in colander for 20 minutes. Rinse eggplant and pat dry. Place in shallow dish.
- Pour 1 cup olive oil over eggplant, tossing to coat. Let stand for 10 minutes; drain.
- Grill over hot coals until brown on both sides.
- Layer eggplant and tomato slices on serving platter. Sprinkle with cheese, olives and capers. Drizzle with green olive oil and wine vinegar. Season with salt and pepper; top with basil.
- Substitute roasted red bell peppers for tomatoes in the winter.
- May prepare eggplant 3 hours before serving.
- Yield: 4 servings.

Green Beans Diablo

6 tablespoons oil
3 tablespoons cider
 vinegar
1/2 teaspoon salt
1/2 teaspoon pepper
2 teaspoons chopped hot
 chilies
1 (16-ounce) can green
 beans, drained
4 hard-boiled eggs,
 chopped
1 tablespoon mayonnaise
2 teaspoons wine vinegar
1 teaspoon prepared
 mustard
4 slices crisp-fried bacon,
 crumbled
1 small onion, minced

- Whisk oil, cider vinegar, salt and pepper together in bowl. Stir in chilies. Stir in green beans.
- Chill, covered, for 2 to 3 hours.
- Combine eggs, mayonnaise, wine vinegar and mustard in bowl; mix well.
- Chill, covered, for 2 to 3 hours.
- Add bacon and onion to green bean mixture, tossing lightly. Spoon into lettuce-lined bowl; top with egg mixture.
- Yield: 4 to 5 servings.

Oriental Jewels

1 (10-ounce) package
 frozen green peas
1 (10-ounce) package
 frozen snow peas
3/4 cup chopped cabbage
1 (8-ounce) can water
 chestnuts, drained,
 sliced
1/2 cup (or less)
 mayonnaise
1/2 cup plain yogurt
1/4 cup relish

- Steam green peas and snow peas in steamer for 1 minute. Let stand until cool. Combine green peas, snow peas, cabbage and water chestnuts in bowl; mix well. Stir in mixture of mayonnaise, yogurt and relish.
- Chill, covered, for 30 minutes.
- Spoon onto lettuce-lined salad plates. Garnish with olives.
- Yield: 8 servings.

Dilly Potato Salad

10 small new potatoes
Salt to taste
1/4 to 1/3 cup Italian salad
  dressing
1/2 cup sour cream
1/2 cup mayonnaise
1/3 cup chopped fresh
  dillweed
1/3 cup chopped celery
Pepper to taste

- Bring new potatoes and salt with enough cold water to cover to a boil in saucepan. Cook for 12 minutes or until tender; drain. Cool for 10 minutes.
- Combine new potatoes with salad dressing in bowl, tossing to coat. Marinate at room temperature for 2 hours or longer, tossing occasionally. Drain, reserving marinade. Chop potatoes into bite-sized pieces.
- Combine potatoes and reserved marinade with mixture of sour cream, mayonnaise and dillweed; mix well. Add celery, salt and pepper; mix well.
- Chill, covered, in refrigerator. Garnish with fresh herbs.
- Yield: 4 to 6 servings.

Hot Parmesan Potato Salad

4 cups sliced cooked
  potatoes
1/2 cup sliced celery
1/4 cup sliced green onions
8 slices crisp-fried bacon,
  crumbled
1/3 cup Italian salad
  dressing
1/2 cup grated Parmesan
  cheese

- Combine potatoes, celery, green onions and bacon in saucepan; mix well. Stir in salad dressing.
- Cook over low heat until heated through, stirring occasionally. Remove from heat.
- Stir in cheese. Garnish with additional grated Parmesan cheese. Serve hot.
- Yield: 4 to 6 servings.

Zesty Potato Salad

12 to 16 ounces red bliss
  potatoes
2$^1/_2$ tablespoons red wine
  vinegar
1 tablespoon whole grain
  mustard
Freshly ground pepper to
  taste
$^1/_4$ cup sliced scallions
1$^1/_2$ tablespoons capers,
  drained
2 tablespoons snipped
  fresh dillweed
2 tablespoons chopped
  Italian parsley
2 tablespoons safflower oil

- Bring potatoes and enough cold water to cover to a boil in saucepan; reduce heat.
- Cook, covered, for 25 minutes or until tender; drain. Cut into thick slices. Place in bowl. Pour mixture of wine vinegar, mustard and pepper over potatoes, tossing to coat.
- Let stand, covered, for 30 minutes.
- Add scallions, capers, dillweed and parsley; mix well. Drizzle safflower oil over mixture, tossing gently to mix.
- Serve at room temperature.
- May be covered and chilled for future use. Bring to room temperature before serving.
- Yield: 4 servings.

Spinach and Strawberry Salad

1 pound fresh spinach,
  torn into bite-sized
  pieces
1 quart strawberries,
  sliced
$^1/_2$ cup oil
$^1/_4$ cup red wine vinegar
1 tablespoon poppy seeds
2 tablespoons sesame
  seeds
$^1/_4$ teaspoon
  Worcestershire sauce
1$^1/_2$ teaspoons grated
  onion
$^1/_4$ cup sugar

- Combine spinach and strawberries in large salad bowl; mix well.
- Pour mixture of oil, wine vinegar, poppy seeds, sesame seeds, Worcestershire sauce, onion and sugar over spinach mixture, tossing to coat.
- Yield: 10 to 12 servings.

Spinach with Honey Dressing

1 tablespoon sesame
  seeds, toasted
6 ounces fresh spinach,
  torn into bite-sized
  pieces
2 tablespoons balsamic
  vinegar
2 tablespoons rice wine
  vinegar
1 tablespoon plus 1
  teaspoon honey
2 to 3 teaspoons Dijon
  mustard
Freshly ground pepper to
  taste
1 cup thickly sliced fresh
  strawberries
1 small red onion, thinly
  sliced

- Cook sesame seeds in heavy skillet over medium-high heat for 2 to 3 minutes or until light brown, stirring constantly. Let stand until cool.
- Place spinach in large salad bowl.
- Whisk balsamic vinegar, rice wine vinegar, honey, Dijon mustard and pepper together in bowl. Pour over spinach; toss lightly.
- Add strawberries, red onion and sesame seeds; toss lightly. Serve immediately.
- Yield: 4 to 5 servings.

Apple and Walnut Spinach Salad

10 ounces fresh spinach
1 cup thinly sliced red
  onion
1 cup chopped walnuts
1 red Delicious apple,
  thinly sliced
3 tablespoons lemon juice
1/2 cup olive oil
2 tablespoons sugar
1 clove of garlic, crushed
1 teaspoon salt

- Combine spinach, red onion, walnuts and apple in salad bowl; mix well.
- Pour mixture of lemon juice, olive oil, sugar, garlic and salt over spinach mixture, tossing to coat.
- Yield: 8 servings.

Hot Spinach Salad

1½ pounds spinach
1 hard-boiled egg, finely chopped
2 teaspoons minced parsley
1 small onion, chopped
¼ teaspoon dry mustard
¼ teaspoon salt
¼ teaspoon pepper
1 tablespoon oil
3 tablespoons red wine vinegar

- Bring spinach and enough water to cover to a boil in saucepan. Boil for 1 to 2 minutes or until tender-crisp; drain. Place in bowl.
- Combine egg, parsley, onion, dry mustard, salt, pepper, oil and wine vinegar in bowl; mix well. Pour over hot spinach; mix well. Serve immediately.
- Yield: 4 servings.

Tabouli

¼ cup finely crushed wheat
4 medium tomatoes, finely chopped
1 bunch scallions, finely chopped
1 teaspoon salt
½ teaspoon allspice
1½ teaspoons dried mint
¼ cup olive oil
¼ cup lemon juice
3 bunches parsley, finely chopped

- Combine wheat, tomatoes, scallions, salt and allspice in bowl; mix well.
- Stir in mint, olive oil and lemon juice. Add parsley; mix well.
- May substitute chopped fresh mint for dried mint.
- Yield: 4 servings.

《◎ ◎》

Make a **Panzanella Salad** of chunks of fresh tomatoes and Italian bread, red onions, black olives and a vinaigrette of olive oil, red wine vinegar and fresh basil.

Mozzarella-Tomato-Olive Salad

12 ounces mozzarella
   cheese, cut into 1/8-inch
   slices
12 fresh basil leaves
1 pound tomatoes, cut
   into 1/8-inch slices
1/2 cup black olives
2/3 cup olive oil
Salt and pepper to taste

- Alternate layers of cheese, basil and tomatoes on 6 salad plates until all ingredients are used, overlapping slightly. Arrange olives in center of each salad.
- Drizzle with olive oil. Season with salt and pepper. Let stand, covered, at room temperature for 30 minutes before serving.
- Yield: 6 servings.

Waldorf Salad Celery Boats

8 large stalks celery
2 tablespoons lemon juice
2 tablespoons oil
1 cup finely chopped red
   apple
3/4 cup finely crumbled
   Roquefort cheese
3/4 cup chopped walnuts
2 tablespoons minced
   fresh parsley
Salt and pepper to taste

- Cut a thin slice with vegetable peeler lengthwise off rounded side of each celery stalk to enable celery to lie open side up.
- Combine remaining ingredients in bowl; mix well. Spoon into celery stalks.
- May cut celery stalks diagonally into 1-inch slices to serve as appetizers.
- May be prepared, covered and chilled 3 hours before serving.
- Yield: 8 servings.

Herb Dressing

1/4 cup cider vinegar
4 teaspoons Dijon mustard
2 tablespoons grated onion
1/4 teaspoon thyme
1/4 teaspoon salt
1/4 teaspoon pepper
1/2 cup olive oil
1/4 cup chopped fresh
   parsley

- Whisk cider vinegar, Dijon mustard, onion, thyme, salt, pepper and olive oil in bowl until thickened. Stir in parsley.
- Chill, covered, in refrigerator.
- Yield: 1 cup.

Mr. O's Salad Dressing

1 cup oil
1 cup cider vinegar
1 cup sugar
1 tablespoon dry mustard

- Whisk oil, cider vinegar, sugar and dry mustard in bowl until blended. Toss with your favorite salad.
- May be used as a marinade.
- Yield: 2 cups.

Roquefort and Sesame Dressing

1 clove of garlic
$1^{1}/_{2}$ teaspoons salt
2 tablespoons red wine vinegar
$2^{1}/_{2}$ tablespoons sesame seeds, toasted
1 tablespoon poppy seeds, toasted
1 tablespoon black mustard seeds, toasted
$1^{1}/_{2}$ teaspoons freshly ground pepper
$3^{1}/_{2}$ tablespoons vegetable or walnut oil
Assorted salad greens
$1/_{2}$ cup crumbled Roquefort cheese
$1/_{2}$ cup walnuts
$1/_{2}$ cup chopped pears

- Mash garlic and salt together in large wooden salad bowl 1 hour before serving. Add wine vinegar; mix well. Stir in hot sesame seeds, poppy seeds and black mustard seeds. Add pepper and oil. Let stand until serving time.
- Place assorted salad greens on top of dressing, tossing to coat. Top with Roquefort cheese, walnuts and pears.
- May substitute $1/_{2}$ cup mandarin orange sections for pears.
- Yield: 4 servings.

For a lighter vinaigrette, use three parts of vinegar or lemon juice
to one part of oil, rather than the more traditional reverse.
Use plenty of herbs and garlic and you will never miss the oil.

MEATS

CASTLE CRAIG • MERIDEN

Easter
Seals

Sweet and Sour Brisket

1 (12-ounce) can beer
1 cup packed whole
  cranberry sauce
1/2 cup catsup
1 (4 to 5-pound) brisket
2 tablespoons oil
1 large onion, sliced

- Combine beer, cranberry sauce and catsup in bowl; mix well and set aside.
- Sear brisket in hot oil in Dutch oven for 5 minutes on each side. Remove brisket.
- Add onion to Dutch oven. Sauté until tender. Place brisket on onion. Pour beer mixture over top.
- Bake at 350 degrees for 3 hours.
- Yield: 6 to 12 servings.

Beef Tenderloin with Mushrooms

1 (5 to 6-pound) beef
  tenderloin
2 tablespoons kosher salt
Coarsely ground pepper
  to taste
Olive oil
2 cloves of garlic, chopped
1 cup red wine
2 tablespoons soy sauce
1 pound fresh mushrooms

- Trim fat from beef. Sprinkle with salt and pepper; rub with olive oil and garlic. Combine with mixture of wine and soy sauce in shallow dish. Marinate in refrigerator for 4 hours to overnight.
- Place on rack in heavy broiler pan. Broil for 20 minutes for medium-rare or until done to taste. Remove beef to platter.
- Sauté mushrooms in drippings in broiler pan. Serve with beef.
- Yield: 12 servings.

For a quick **Beef Stroganoff**, brown 1 pound of sirloin steak strips with 1 chopped onion, and stir in 1 cup of water and 1 package of mushroom gravy mix. Simmer for 30 minutes. Serve over rice or noodles with sour cream.

Sauerbraten

1 (4-pound) beef rump
   roast
6 carrots, peeled, sliced
3 medium onions, sliced
1 tablespoon sugar
1 quart buttermilk
1 teaspoon mustard seeds
4 whole cloves
20 black peppercorns
4 bay leaves
Oil for browning
1 envelope onion soup
   mix or brown gravy mix
1 teaspoon cornstarch
1 teaspoon sugar
Evaporated milk

- Combine beef, carrots, onions, 1 tablespoon sugar, buttermilk, mustard seeds, cloves, peppercorns and bay leaves in shallow dish. Marinate, covered, in refrigerator for 4 or 5 days, turning beef once a day.
- Remove beef from marinade and pat dry; reserve marinade. Brown roast on all sides in oil in 6-quart saucepan. Add marinade. Simmer, covered, for 4 to 5 hours.
- Remove beef to serving plate. Strain cooking juices into saucepan. Stir in soup mix. Boil for 5 minutes.
- Combine cornstarch and 1 teaspoon sugar with enough evaporated milk to blend in bowl. Stir into boiling juices. Cook until thickened, stirring constantly.
- Slice beef. Serve with gravy.
- Yield: 8 servings.

Carpet Bag Steaks

6 (1½-inch thick) beef
   tenderloin steaks
²/₃ to ³/₄ cup small fresh
   or canned oysters
1 tablespoon butter,
   chopped
1 teaspoon salt
¹/₄ teaspoon pepper
Melted butter
Salt and pepper to taste

- Cut a pocket into the side of each steak with sharp knife. Combine oysters, chopped butter, salt and pepper in bowl. Stuff into pockets; secure with small skewers and string if necessary.
- Brush steaks with melted butter; place on rack in broiler pan. Broil 6 inches from heat source for 6 minutes on each side for rare, for 8 minutes for medium and for 10 minutes or more for well done. Adjust seasonings to taste.
- Yield: 6 servings.

Mushroom Steaks

8 ounces fresh
  mushrooms, sliced
1 tablespoon butter
3 tablespoons chopped
  onion
2 tablespoons flour
1¹/₂ cups half and half
1 teaspoon soy sauce
1 teaspoon grated onion
Salt and pepper to taste
1 tablespoon butter
4 (1¹/₂ pounds) top sirloin
  steaks

- Sauté mushrooms in 1 tablespoon butter in heavy saucepan until light brown. Add chopped onion. Sauté until onion is tender.
- Stir in flour. Add half and half gradually. Cook mixture until thickened, stirring constantly. Add soy sauce, grated onion, salt and pepper.
- Brown 1 tablespoon butter in skillet. Add steaks. Cook until steaks are brown on both sides; reduce heat. Simmer, covered, for several minutes.
- Add mushroom sauce to skillet. Simmer until steaks are done to taste. Garnish with red or green bell pepper strips.
- Yield: 4 servings.

Beef Bourguignon

6 slices bacon, chopped
3 pounds lean beef cubes
Salt and pepper to taste
¹/₄ cup flour
2 tablespoons butter
2 carrots, sliced
2 medium onions, sliced
3 cups Burgundy wine
2 cups beef stock or
  consommé
3 cloves of garlic, minced
1 pound mushrooms,
  thickly sliced
¹/₄ cup butter
2 (16-ounce) cans small
  white onions, drained
2 tablespoons chopped
  parsley

- Fry bacon in skillet until crisp; remove bacon, reserving drippings in skillet.
- Season beef with salt and pepper; coat with flour. Brown on all sides in drippings in skillet. Remove beef to baking dish; mix with bacon. Add 2 tablespoons butter, carrots and sliced onions to skillet. Sauté until golden brown. Add to baking dish.
- Add wine, beef stock and garlic to drippings in skillet, stirring to deglaze. Cook until heated through. Pour over beef. Bake, covered, at 325 degrees for 3 hours or until beef is tender.
- Sauté mushrooms in ¹/₄ cup butter in skillet for 5 minutes. Add canned onions. Cook until heated through. Stir into beef mixture. Sprinkle with parsley.
- Yield: 8 to 10 servings.

Beef Oriental with Rice

1/4 cup soy sauce
1 tablespoon sugar
2 tablespoons dry sherry
2 tablespoons oil
1/2 to 3/4 teaspoon ginger
2 cloves of garlic, minced
1 pound top sirloin beef
   steak
2 tablespoons oil
2 medium carrots, cut
   into 1-inch julienne
   strips
2 stalks celery, sliced
   diagonally 1/4 inch thick
1 medium onion, cut into
   wedges
1 (6-ounce) package
   frozen pea pods,
   thawed, drained
1 (8-ounce) can sliced
   water chestnuts, drained
1 tablespoon cornstarch
1/2 cup cold water

- Combine soy sauce, sugar, wine, 2 tablespoons oil, ginger and garlic in large bowl; mix well. Cut steak into thin strips.
- Add steak to marinade, coating well. Marinate, covered, for 30 minutes or longer. Drain, reserving marinade.
- Heat 2 tablespoons oil in large skillet or wok over medium-high heat until oil ripples. Add steak. Stir-fry for 2 minutes. Add marinade. Cook until marinade is bubbly.
- Add carrots. Cook, covered, for 2 to 3 minutes or until carrots are tender-crisp. Add celery, onion, pea pods and water chestnuts. Cook for 1 minute.
- Stir in mixture of cornstarch and water. Cook until thickened, stirring constantly. Serve over rice.
- Yield: 4 or 5 servings.

Five-Hour Beef Stew

4 potatoes, peeled
5 carrots, peeled
5 stalks celery
1 large onion
2 pounds stew beef
1 (10-ounce) can tomato
   soup
1 can beef bouillon

- Cut potatoes, carrots, celery and onion into 1-inch pieces. Combine with stew beef, soup and bouillon in baking dish; mix well.
- Bake at 300 degrees for 5 hours, stirring occasionally.
- Make soup of leftovers by adding 1 large can whole tomatoes, 1 cup water, 1 can beef bouillon and 1/2 package frozen mixed vegetables or leftover vegetables; simmer for 20 minutes.
- Yield: 6 servings.

Roast Veal Danube

1 (4-pound) boned veal
  roast, rolled, tied
6 slices bacon
1 teaspoon salt
1/2 teaspoon pepper
1/2 cup melted butter
1/2 cup white wine

- Place roast on rack in roasting pan; top with bacon. Sprinkle with salt and pepper.
- Roast at 325 degrees for 2 hours, basting frequently with mixture of butter and wine.
- Yield: 8 servings.

Veal Française

8 ounces thin veal scallops
1/4 cup flour
1 teaspoon salt
1/4 teaspoon pepper
5 to 6 tablespoons
  unsalted butter
3 eggs, beaten
2 tablespoons dry white
  wine
1 tablespoon fresh lemon
  juice

- Pound veal scallops very thin with meat mallet. Coat with mixture of flour, salt and pepper, shaking off excess.
- Melt butter in saucepan over low heat. Cook until butter foams; remove from heat. Skim off foam. Spoon off clear butter, leaving solids in bottom of saucepan. Measure 1/4 cup clarified butter.
- Heat clarified butter in large skillet over medium-high heat until butter ripples. Dip veal into egg. Place in single layer in oil in skillet.
- Sauté for 3 minutes or until golden brown on both sides. Remove and arrange in slightly overlapping layer on warm platter.
- Add wine and lemon juice to skillet, stirring to deglaze. Bring to a boil. Pour over veal; garnish with lemon slices. Serve immediately.
- Yield: 2 servings.

Veal in Paprika Cream

1 large onion, chopped
1 small clove of garlic, chopped
2 tablespoons oil
1 teaspoon salt
2 tablespoons paprika
1 large tomato, peeled, chopped
1 1/2 pounds veal round steak, cubed
2 cups sour cream
1 (8-ounce) package egg noodles, cooked

- Sauté onion and garlic in oil in saucepan until golden brown. Stir in salt and paprika. Add tomato and veal.
- Simmer, covered, for 45 minutes or until veal is tender. Stir in sour cream. Cook just until heated through; do not boil.
- Serve with noodles; garnish with minced parsley.
- Yield: 6 servings.

Mexican Lasagna

1 pound ground beef
1 medium onion, chopped
3 tablespoons cumin
2 teaspoons chili powder
1/2 teaspoon paprika
Oregano and salt to taste
1 tablespoon white pepper
1 egg, beaten
15 ounces ricotta cheese
2 jalapeño peppers, chopped
3 (10-inch) tortillas
1 (16-ounce) can refried beans
1 1/2 cups shredded Cheddar cheese
1 cup sliced black olives

- Cook ground beef in skillet over medium heat, stirring until partially cooked; drain. Add onion, cumin, chili powder, paprika, oregano, salt and white pepper; mix well. Cook until ground beef is brown and crumbly.
- Combine egg, ricotta cheese and jalapeño pepper in small bowl; mix well.
- Layer 1 tortilla, refried beans, ground beef mixture, 1 tortilla, ricotta cheese mixture, remaining tortilla and Cheddar cheese in baking dish.
- Bake, covered, at 350 degrees for 15 minutes. Bake, uncovered, for 10 minutes longer. Sprinkle with sliced olives. Serve with salsa and sour cream.
- This recipe is from Ben Sauer, Cook at the Foxwood Casino.
- Yield: 4 to 8 servings.

Herbed Meat Loaf with Spinach

1 pound lean ground beef
8 ounces ground pork
1¹/₂ cups finely chopped
 fresh spinach
³/₄ cup bread crumbs
¹/₂ cup shelled pistachios
3 cloves of garlic, minced
¹/₂ teaspoon dried thyme
¹/₂ teaspoon dried rosemary
1 teaspoon ground nutmeg
1 teaspoon salt
¹/₂ teaspoon pepper
2 eggs, slightly beaten
2 tablespoons cream
1 tablespoon Dijon mustard
6 slices bacon (optional)
5 ounces fresh
 mushrooms, sliced
1 tablespoon olive oil
1 jar mushroom gravy

- Combine ground beef, ground pork, spinach, bread crumbs, pistachios, garlic, thyme, rosemary, nutmeg, salt and pepper in bowl; mix well.
- Combine eggs, cream and mustard in small bowl. Add to ground beef mixture; mix well. Shape into loaf in loaf pan; top with bacon. Bake at 350 degrees for 50 to 60 minutes or until cooked through.
- Sauté mushrooms in oil in skillet until golden brown. Stir in gravy.
- Remove meat loaf to serving plate. Serve with mushroom gravy.
- Yield: 6 servings.

Italian Meat Loaf Whirl

2 pounds ground beef
2 eggs
1 cup fresh bread crumbs
2 tablespoons minced
 onion
1 teaspoon oregano
1 teaspoon garlic salt
¹/₈ teaspoon pepper
1 (8-ounce) can tomato
 sauce
3 ounces salami, thinly
 sliced
8 ounces mozzarella,
 shredded

- Mix ground beef, eggs, bread crumbs, onion, oregano, garlic salt, pepper and half the tomato sauce in bowl.
- Shape into 10x16-inch rectangle on waxed paper. Arrange salami over ground beef mixture, leaving 1-inch edges; sprinkle with cheese. Roll from narrow side as for jelly roll, lifting with waxed paper; press edge and ends to seal.
- Place seam side down in loaf pan. Bake at 350 degrees for 1 hour; drain. Remove to baking dish. Top with remaining tomato sauce. Bake for 15 minutes longer. Let stand for 15 minutes before serving.
- Yield: 8 servings.

Ribbon Meat Loaf

2 pounds lean ground beef
1 small onion, minced
1 cup milk
1 teaspoon salt
Pepper to taste
1 (8-ounce) package
    herb-seasoned stuffing
    mix

- Combine ground beef, onion, milk, salt and pepper in bowl; mix well. Spread 1/3 of the ground beef mixture in 5x9-inch loaf pan. Prepare stuffing mix using package directions. Layer stuffing mixture and remaining ground beef mixture 1/2 at a time in prepared pan.
- Bake at 350 degrees for 1 1/4 hours. Remove to serving plate.
- Yield: 8 servings.

Mexicali Pie with Cornmeal Crust

6 slices bacon
2 tablespoons cornmeal
1 cup flour
3 to 4 tablespoons water
1 pound ground beef
1 cup drained canned
    whole kernel corn
1 cup drained canned
    black beans
1/4 cup chopped onion
1/4 cup chopped green bell
    pepper
1/4 cup cornmeal
1/2 teaspoon oregano
1/2 teaspoon chili powder
1 (8-ounce) can tomato
    sauce
1 teaspoon salt
1 teaspoon pepper
1 egg
1/4 cup low-fat milk
1/2 teaspoon
    Worcestershire sauce
1 1/2 cups shredded
    Cheddar cheese
4 stuffed olives, sliced

- Fry bacon in skillet until crumbly. Remove and crumble bacon into large pieces; drain skillet, reserving 1/3 cup drippings. Chill reserved drippings until firm.
- Mix 2 tablespoons cornmeal and flour in bowl. Cut in chilled bacon drippings until crumbly. Sprinkle with water; stir with fork to form dough. Roll on floured surface; fit into 12-inch pie plate. Trim edge.
- Brown ground beef in large skillet, stirring until crumbly; drain. Stir in corn, beans, onion, green pepper, 1/4 cup cornmeal, oregano, chili powder, tomato sauce, salt and pepper.
- Spoon into pastry-lined pie plate. Bake at 425 degrees for 25 minutes.
- Combine egg, milk, Worcestershire sauce and cheese in bowl; mix well. Pour over ground beef mixture. Top with bacon and olives. Bake for 5 minutes longer or until cheese melts. Let stand for 10 minutes before serving.
- Yield: 6 servings.

Cajun Stuffed Peppers

6 green bell peppers
1 pound ground beef
1/4 cup butter
2 yellow onions, chopped
2 green onions, chopped
2 cloves of garlic, finely
  chopped
1/2 teaspoon instant beef
  bouillon
2 pinches of basil
3 or 4 dashes of Tabasco
  sauce
1/2 teaspoon chili powder
1 (16-ounce) can Italian
  stewed tomatoes
1/2 cup rice, cooked
1/2 cup shredded Cheddar
  cheese
1/2 cup grated Parmesan
  cheese
1/8 teaspoon cayenne
  pepper

- Cut off tops of peppers, discarding seeds. Boil in water in saucepan for 8 minutes or until tender; drain.
- Brown ground beef in butter in skillet, stirring until crumbly; drain all but 2 tablespoons drippings. Add yellow onions, green onions and garlic. Sauté until tender.
- Add beef bouillon, basil, Tabasco sauce, chili powder, stewed tomatoes, rice, Cheddar cheese, Parmesan cheese and cayenne pepper; mix well.
- Stuff mixture into peppers; arrange in baking dish. Add enough water to just cover bottom of dish.
- Bake at 350 degrees for 25 to 30 minutes.
- Yield: 6 servings.

Orange Marmalade Ham

1 (4 to 5-pound) cooked
  boneless ham
1/4 cup orange marmalade
1/4 cup packed brown
  sugar
1 teaspoon dry mustard
Ground cloves and
  nutmeg to taste
1 to 2 teaspoons whole
  cloves

- Place ham on rack in roasting pan. Bake, uncovered, at 325 degrees for 45 minutes.
- Combine marmalade, brown sugar, dry mustard, ground cloves and nutmeg in bowl; mix well.
- Score top of ham 1/4 inch deep in diamond pattern. Insert 1 whole clove in each diamond. Brush with marmalade mixture.
- Bake for 15 to 30 minutes or until 135 degrees on meat thermometer. Remove to large serving platter; garnish with orange slices and parsley.
- Yield: 12 servings.

Brandied Ham Steaks

2 tablespoons butter
2 (1-pound) ham steaks,
   1/2 inch thick
3 tablespoons brandy

- Heat butter in skillet over medium heat until foam subsides. Add ham steaks. Brown for 3 to 4 minutes on each side; remove to warm serving plate; drain skillet.
- Add brandy. Cook over high heat for 1 to 2 minutes, stirring to deglaze skillet. Pour over steaks. Serve immediately.
- Yield: 4 servings.

Ham Loaf

1 1/2 pounds smoked ham
1 1/2 pounds pork
2 cups fresh bread crumbs
1/2 cup milk
1 cup packed brown sugar
2 tablespoons dry mustard
1/4 cup water
1 cup whipping cream,
   whipped, or 1 cup sour
   cream
Horseradish to taste

- Ask butcher to grind ham and pork together. Combine ham mixture with bread crumbs and milk in bowl; mix well. Shape into loaf in 8x12-inch baking pan.
- Combine brown sugar, dry mustard and water in bowl; mix well. Pour over ham loaf.
- Bake at 325 degrees for 2 hours, basting every 30 minutes and adding boiling water if needed.
- Mix whipped cream with horseradish to taste in bowl. Serve with ham loaf.
- Yield: 8 servings.

Baste ham steak with a mixture of 1/4 cup mustard, 1/2 cup
packed brown sugar, 2 tablespoons pineapple juice and
a dash of ground cloves while grilling. Add pineapple slices
about 5 minutes before removing from grill.

Ham and Cheese Strudel

2 cups finely chopped
  cooked smoked ham
1 cup shredded Swiss
  cheese
1 (4-ounce) can
  mushroom stems and
  pieces, drained
1 egg, slightly beaten
1/4 cup sliced green onions
2 (8-count) cans crescent
  rolls
Melted butter or cream
1/2 cup sour cream
1/3 cup melted butter
1/2 cup mayonnaise
2 tablespoons dry mustard
1/2 teaspoon sugar

- Combine ham, cheese, mushrooms, egg and green onions in bowl; mix well.
- Separate roll dough into 8 portions; press perforations to seal. Spoon ham mixture into center of squares. Pull up corners of dough to enclose filling; press to seal.
- Place on lightly greased baking sheet. Brush tops with butter or cream. Bake at 350 to 375 degrees for 15 to 20 minutes or until golden brown.
- Combine sour cream, 1/3 cup melted butter, mayonnaise, dry mustard and sugar in saucepan. Cook until heated through, stirring constantly. Serve with strudels.
- Yield: 8 servings.

Pork Roast with Apple Plum Sauce

1 (5-pound) center-cut
  pork loin roast
Salt and pepper to taste
1 (17-ounce) can whole
  purple plums
1 (15-ounce) jar
  applesauce
1/4 teaspoon pumpkin pie
  spice
1/8 teaspoon cinnamon

- Sprinkle pork with salt and pepper; place on rack in shallow roasting pan.
- Roast at 325 degrees for 30 to 35 minutes per pound or to 170 degrees on meat thermometer.
- Drain plums, reserving 1/4 cup syrup; discard pits. Process plums with reserved syrup in blender at medium speed for 1 minute.
- Combine plum purée with applesauce, pumpkin pie spice and cinnamon in saucepan. Heat to serving temperature. Serve over sliced pork.
- Yield: 12 servings.

Pork Loin with Pineapple Glaze

1 (8-ounce) can sliced
  pineapple
1 teaspoon dry mustard
1/2 teaspoon ginger
1/2 teaspoon paprika
1 tablespoon brown sugar
1 tablespoon lemon juice
2 teaspoons cornstarch
1 (1 1/2-pound) pork loin

- Drain pineapple, reserving 1/2 cup juice. Combine reserved juice with dry mustard, ginger, paprika, brown sugar, lemon juice and cornstarch in saucepan; mix well. Cook until thickened, stirring constantly.
- Place pork on rack in roasting pan. Brush with part of the pineapple glaze. Roast at 350 degrees for 1 1/4 hours or to 160 degrees on meat thermometer, brushing with glaze several times and turning once to brush bottom side.
- Let stand for 5 minutes. Slice pork cross grain. Arrange pineapple slices around pork to serve.
- Yield: 4 to 6 servings.

Fruit-Stuffed Loin of Pork

1 (4-pound) boneless pork
  loin roast
1 cup pitted prunes
1 cup dried apricots
1 clove of garlic, slivered
Salt and pepper to taste
1/2 cup unsalted butter,
  softened
1 tablespoon thyme
1 cup Madeira
1 tablespoon molasses

- Ask butcher to prepare pork roast with pocket for stuffing. Push prunes and apricots into pocket with handle of wooden spoon, alternating fruits. Cut deep slits in roast with point of sharp knife. Place slivers of garlic in slits. Tie roast with string.
- Rub with salt and pepper. Place in shallow roasting pan. Rub with butter; sprinkle with thyme. Pour mixture of wine and molasses over roast.
- Roast at 350 degrees on middle rack of oven for 1 1/2 hours, basting frequently; do not overcook.
- Remove to serving platter. Let stand, loosely covered with foil, for 15 to 20 minutes. Cut into thin slices; spoon juices over slices.
- Yield: 12 servings.

Dill and Caraway Pork

4 (12-ounce) pork
   tenderloins
2 tablespoons olive oil
1/2 cup reduced-sodium
   chicken stock
2 tablespoons Dijon
   mustard
1/4 cup whipping or heavy
   cream
2 teaspoons caraway seeds
1 tablespoon chopped
   fresh dill

- Brown pork on all sides in olive oil in large skillet over high heat. Add mixture of chicken stock and mustard.
- Cook, covered, for 5 minutes; turn pork over. Add cream and caraway seeds. Cook, uncovered, for 10 minutes longer.
- Remove pork to serving platter. Cook pan juices until thickened enough to coat spoon. Stir in dill.
- Slice pork. Spoon sauce over slices.
- Yield: 6 to 12 servings.

Pork Tenderloins Victoria

2 pounds pork tenderloins
1 cup flour
6 tablespoons butter
2 Granny Smith apples,
   peeled, sliced
1 small and 1/2 medium
   Spanish onion, sliced
1/4 cup packed brown
   sugar
1 tablespoon cinnamon
1/2 tablespoon nutmeg
1/2 teaspoon salt
1/4 teaspoon white pepper
2 tablespoons butter

- Remove fat and silver skin from pork tenderloins. Slice into twelve 3/4-inch medallions. Pound thin with meat mallet. Coat with flour.
- Heat 6 tablespoons butter in large skillet over medium-high heat. Add pork medallions, apples and onions. Cook for 2 to 3 minutes; turn medallions over. Sprinkle with brown sugar, cinnamon, nutmeg, salt and white pepper.
- Cook, covered, for 3 to 4 minutes, stirring constantly and adding remaining 2 tablespoons butter. Simmer until reduced to desired consistency. Stir in 1/4 cup water if needed.
- Place pork on serving plates; spoon pan juices over top. Serve with rice.
- Yield: 3 to 4 servings.

Rhone Pork Chops

1 pound sauerkraut
1 (15-ounce) jar
  applesauce
1 tablespoon brown sugar
8 (1-inch thick) loin pork
  chops
1/4 cup white wine

- Rinse sauerkraut in cold water and drain. Combine with applesauce and brown sugar in bowl; mix well. Spread in shallow baking dish.
- Sauté pork chops in skillet until golden brown on both sides. Arrange on sauerkraut. Pour wine over top.
- Bake, covered with foil, at 350 degrees for 1 hour.
- Yield: 8 servings.

Pork with Cider Sauce

1 1/2 pounds lean boneless
  pork, cut into 1-inch
  cubes
1/3 cup flour
1/3 cup canola oil
2 large carrots, sliced
1 small onion, sliced
1/2 teaspoon rosemary
1 bay leaf
1 teaspoon salt
1/2 teaspoon pepper
1 1/2 cups apple cider or
  apple juice

- Coat pork with flour. Brown on all sides in heated oil in large skillet. Remove and drain pork; drain skillet.
- Place pork in baking dish. Add carrots, onion, rosemary, bay leaf, salt and pepper; mix well.
- Add cider to skillet, stirring to deglaze. Pour into baking dish.
- Bake at 325 degrees for 2 hours or until pork is tender; discard bay leaf.
- Yield: 4 servings.

Make an **Easy Pork Barbecue Sauce** of 1 cup catsup, 1 cup apple jelly, 2 tablespoons vinegar and 2 teaspoons chili powder. Simmer sauce for 1 minute before pouring over pork roast.

Pork and Pepper with Pineapple Rice

1 (8-ounce) can crushed pineapple
1/4 cup hot water
2/3 cup uncooked instant rice
12 ounces lean boneless pork, cut into thin strips
1 medium green bell pepper, cut into thin strips
1/3 cup cold water
1 tablespoon soy sauce
2 teaspoons cornstarch
1 teaspoon grated orange rind
1/4 teaspoon pepper

• Combine undrained pineapple and hot water in 1-quart glass dish. Microwave on High for 1 1/2 to 3 minutes or until mixture boils. Stir in rice; cover. Set aside.

• Combine pork and green pepper in 1 1/2-quart glass dish. Microwave on High for 4 to 5 minutes or until pork is no longer pink, stirring once; drain.

• Mix cold water, soy sauce, cornstarch, orange rind and pepper in 1-cup glass measure. Pour over pork.

• Microwave on High for 1 to 3 minutes or until sauce is thickened and pork is tender. Serve over pineapple rice.

• Yield: 4 servings.

Barbecued Lamb

4 cloves of garlic, crushed
1/4 cup honey
1/3 cup soy sauce
2 tablespoons oil
2 tablespoons lemon juice
1/3 cup hot water
1 leg of lamb, butterflied

• Combine garlic, honey, soy sauce, oil and lemon juice with hot water in shallow dish; mix well. Let stand until cool.

• Trim fat from lamb. Add to marinade. Marinate, covered, in refrigerator for 4 hours to overnight.

• Remove lamb from marinade. Grill over hot coals for 5 minutes on each side to sear. Place in baking dish.

• Bake at 400 degrees for 15 minutes or until done to taste. Serve with spinach salad, brown rice, garlic bread and strong red wine.

• Yield: 8 servings.

POULTRY

CAPITOL OVERLOOKING BUSHNELL PARK • HARTFORD

Easter Seals

Baked Chicken in Asparagus Sauce

3/4 cup bread crumbs or finely crushed crackers
2 tablespoons grated Romano or Parmesan cheese
1 tablespoon parsley flakes
1/2 teaspoon salt
1 (2 1/2 to 3-pound) chicken, cut into 8 pieces
1/3 cup melted butter
1/2 cup butter
1 (10-ounce) package frozen cut asparagus, thawed, drained
1/2 cup sliced onion
1 (4-ounce) can mushroom stems and pieces, drained
1 teaspoon Italian herb seasoning
1/2 teaspoon garlic salt

- Combine bread crumbs, cheese, parsley flakes and salt in bowl. Rinse chicken and pat dry. Dip in 1/3 cup melted butter and coat with crumb mixture. Arrange skin side up in 9x13-inch baking pan.
- Bake at 375 degrees on center oven rack for 1 hour to 1 1/4 hours or until chicken is tender.
- Melt 1/2 cup butter in saucepan. Add asparagus, onion, mushrooms, herb seasoning and garlic salt; mix well. Cook, covered, over low heat for 5 to 10 minutes or until asparagus is tender. Serve over chicken.
- Yield: 4 servings.

※

Marinate chicken breast filets in a mixture of 1/2 cup soy sauce, minced garlic, 3/4 teaspoon ginger, 2 tablespoons sugar and 1 ounce sherry for 4 to 6 hours. Grill for 15 minutes.

Chicken Cacciatore with Orzo

2 (3-pound) chickens
1 onion, sliced
2 carrots, sliced
1 ounce parsley, chopped
2 stalks celery with tops,
  chopped
Salt and pepper to taste
3 onions, sliced
8 ounces fresh
  mushrooms, sliced
2 cloves of garlic, chopped
1/2 ounce parsley, chopped
1/2 teaspoon oregano
1/4 teaspoon crushed red
  pepper
1/4 cup olive oil or
  blended oil
1 (15-ounce) can Italian
  style tomato sauce
1 pound orzo, cooked

- Rinse chickens and pat dry. Combine with 1 onion, carrots, 1 ounce parsley and celery in large soup pot. Add enough water to just cover chicken.
- Cook over low heat until chicken begins to come from bone. Remove chickens from soup pot; cool to room temperature.
- Bone chicken; discard skin and bones. Reserve meaty pieces for cacciatore; add smaller pieces to soup pot. Heat to serving temperature.
- Sauté 3 onions, mushrooms, garlic, 1/2 ounce parsley, oregano, red pepper and salt and pepper to taste in olive oil in large skillet. Stir in tomato sauce and reserved chicken. Simmer for 15 to 20 minutes. Place orzo in serving bowls. Ladle soup over orzo. Serve with cacciatore.
- Yield: 12 servings.

Chicken Amalfi

1 pound chicken breast
  filets
Flour
2 tablespoons olive oil
3 ounces sun-dried
  tomatoes, chopped
1 (8-ounce) can artichoke
  hearts, drained
1 clove of garlic, minced
Juice of 1/2 lemon
1/4 cup white wine
1/4 cup chicken stock
1 tablespoon balsamic
  vinegar
Salt and pepper to taste

- Rinse chicken and pat dry. Pound 1/4 inch thick with meat mallet. Cut into 12 pieces. Coat lightly with flour.
- Sauté in olive oil in skillet for 5 minutes, turning once. Add tomatoes and artichoke hearts. Cook for 1 minute. Add garlic. Cook for 1 minute.
- Add lemon juice and wine. Cook until reduced by 1/2. Add chicken stock. Cook for 3 minutes or until thickened to desired consistency. Stir in vinegar. Bring to a boil; reduce heat. Simmer for 1 to 2 minutes. Season with salt and pepper. Serve over pasta.
- Yield: 4 servings.

Chicken with Artichokes

2 (18-ounce) cans
  marinated artichoke
  hearts
6 chicken breast filets
1/2 cup grated Parmesan
  cheese
1 1/2 cups seasoned bread
  crumbs
1/2 cup olive oil
1 cup white cooking wine
1/2 cup chopped parsley
1/2 cup chopped scallions
4 or 5 cloves of garlic,
  crushed
8 ounces Muenster
  cheese, sliced

- Spread artichokes with marinade in 9x13-inch baking dish.
- Rinse chicken and pat dry. Dip into water; coat with mixture of Parmesan cheese and bread crumbs. Arrange over artichokes.
- Bake at 400 degrees for 30 minutes; reduce oven temperature to 350 degrees.
- Combine olive oil, wine, parsley, scallions and garlic in jar; shake to mix well. Pour evenly over chicken.
- Bake for 20 minutes longer. Top with Muenster cheese. Let stand just until cheese melts. Serve immediately.
- Yield: 6 servings.

Chicken à la Charlotte

1 1/2 cups sour cream
2 tablespoons
  Worcestershire sauce
1/2 teaspoon paprika
2 tablespoons lemon juice
1 1/2 teaspoons garlic
  powder
Salt and pepper to taste
3 whole chicken breasts,
  boned, skinned, cut
  into halves
2 cups bread crumbs
1/2 cup melted butter

- Combine sour cream, Worcestershire sauce, paprika, lemon juice, garlic powder, salt and pepper in bowl; mix well. Rinse chicken and pat dry. Coat well with sour cream mixture.
- Arrange chicken in shallow dish. Spoon remaining sour cream mixture over top. Chill, covered, overnight.
- Scrape excess sour cream mixture from chicken; coat with bread crumbs. Arrange in single layer in baking dish; drizzle with butter.
- Bake at 350 degrees for 30 minutes or until chicken is tender.
- Yield: 4 to 6 servings.

Chicken à la Cheddar

10 ounces sharp Cheddar
   cheese
4 whole chicken breasts,
   boned, skinned, cut
   into halves
2 eggs, beaten
3/4 cup bread crumbs
Butter
1/2 cup chopped onion
1/2 cup chopped green bell
   pepper
1/4 cup butter
2 tablespoons flour
1 teaspoon salt
1/4 teaspoon pepper
3/4 cup water
2 cups cooked white rice
1 cup cooked wild rice
1 1/2 cups sliced mushrooms
1/4 cup butter
3 tablespoons flour
1 chicken bouillon cube
1/2 cup boiling water
1/2 cup milk
1/3 cup dry white wine

- Cut cheese into 8 sticks. Rinse chicken and pat dry. Pound 1/4 inch thick with meat mallet. Roll each piece of chicken around 1 stick of cheese; secure with wooden picks.
- Dip rolls into eggs; coat with bread crumbs. Brown on all sides in butter in skillet; remove to platter.
- Sauté onion and green pepper in 1/4 cup butter in skillet. Stir in 2 tablespoons flour, salt and pepper. Stir in 3/4 cup water gradually. Cook until thickened, stirring constantly. Add rice; mix well.
- Spoon into 8x12-inch baking dish; top with chicken rolls. Bake at 400 degrees for 20 minutes.
- Sauté mushrooms in 1/4 cup butter in skillet. Stir in 3 tablespoons flour and bouillon dissolved in 1/2 cup boiling water. Add milk. Cook until thickened, stirring constantly. Add wine. Cook until heated through. Serve over chicken.
- Yield: 8 servings.

Chicken Dijon Bake

1/3 cup mayonnaise
2 tablespoons Dijon
   mustard
1/2 teaspoon wine vinegar
1/4 teaspoon celery seeds
1/4 teaspoon tarragon
1 to 2 pounds chicken
   breast filets
1/3 to 1/2 cup bread crumbs

- Combine mayonnaise, mustard, wine vinegar, celery seeds and tarragon in small bowl; mix well.
- Rinse chicken and pat dry. Coat with mayonnaise mixture; coat with bread crumbs.
- Arrange in 9x13-inch baking dish. Bake at 350 degrees for 25 to 30 minutes or until chicken is tender. Serve with rice pilaf and leafy green vegetable.
- Yield: 3 to 5 servings.

Chicken with Cognac Cream Sauce

6 chicken breasts
Flour
Olive oil
2 cups chicken broth
Chopped garlic and fresh
  basil to taste
1 large can marinated
  artichoke hearts
1 (8-ounce) jar sun-dried
  tomatoes packed in
  olive oil
Red pepper flakes to taste
1/2 cup heavy cream
1/4 cup Cognac
1 1/2 pounds penne, cooked

- Cut chicken into bite-sized pieces; rinse and pat dry. Coat with flour. Sauté in olive oil in large skillet until golden brown; remove chicken
- Add chicken broth, garlic, basil, undrained artichoke hearts and undrained sun-dried tomatoes. Cook until reduced to 2 cups. Add chicken with pepper flakes, cream and Cognac. Cook until heated through.
- Serve with pasta. Garnish with grated Parmesan cheese.
- Yield: 6 servings.

Chicken Florentine

4 chicken breasts
Flour
Oil for sautéing
1/2 cup butter
1 tablespoon water
2 tablespoons lemon juice
3 tablespoons sherry
Cooked spinach

- Rinse chicken and pat dry. Coat with flour. Sauté in oil in skillet until light brown on both sides.
- Melt butter in small skillet. Stir in water, lemon juice and wine. Simmer for several minutes.
- Arrange chicken over spinach; spoon sauce over top.
- Yield: 4 servings.

Baked or roasted chicken has fewer calories than stewed chicken. Remove skin to further reduce calories.

Fruited Chicken

6 chicken breast filets
Corn flake crumbs
Mrs. Dash seasoning to
 taste
1 small green bell pepper,
 cut into strips
1 small can pineapple
 chunks
1 small can sliced peaches
1 small jar maraschino
 cherries
1/2 cup duck sauce

- Rinse chicken and pat dry. Shake in mixture of corn flakes and seasoning in plastic bag. Arrange in 9x13-inch baking dish. Arrange green pepper slices over chicken.
- Drain pineapple chunks, peaches and cherries, reserving pineapple juice, peach juice and some of the cherry juice. Place pineapple, peaches and cherries over chicken. Combine reserved juices with duck sauce in bowl; mix well. Pour over chicken and fruit.
- Bake, covered with foil, at 350 degrees for 15 minutes. Bake, uncovered, for 15 minutes longer.
- May substitute other fruit for fruit listed.
- Yield: 4 to 6 servings.

Chicken with Lobster Sauce

8 chicken breast filets
Salt and pepper to taste
1/4 cup butter
2 tablespoons sherry
12 ounces fresh
 mushrooms, sliced
2 tablespoons flour
1 1/2 cups chicken stock
Tomato paste to taste
2 (10-ounce) packages
 frozen lobster tails

- Rinse chicken and pat dry. Sprinkle with salt and pepper. Sauté in butter in large skillet until golden brown. Drizzle with wine. Remove to shallow baking dish. Bake, covered, at 300 degrees for 1 hour or until tender.
- Sauté mushrooms in drippings in skillet. Stir in flour and chicken stock. Cook until thickened, stirring constantly. Stir in tomato paste, salt and pepper. Simmer for 15 minutes longer.
- Remove lobster meat from tails; cut into bite-sized pieces. Add to sauce. Simmer until lobster is cooked through.
- Arrange chicken on serving platter. Spoon sauce over top; place lobster meat on top.
- Yield: 6 to 8 servings.

Chicken with Lemon and Brandy

6 chicken breast filets
1/2 cup flour
1 teaspoon oregano
Salt and pepper to taste
Oil for sautéing
1/4 cup lemon juice
1/4 cup brandy
2 tablespoons chopped
  parsley

- Rinse chicken and pat dry. Shake with mixture of flour, oregano, salt and pepper in plastic bag.
- Sauté in oil in sauté pan for 10 minutes or until golden brown; do not overcook. Decrease heat.
- Stir in lemon juice. Cook until reduced to desired consistency. Increase heat. Stir in brandy. Ignite brandy; allow flames to die down. Sprinkle with parsley; garnish with lemon twists.
- Yield: 6 servings.

Marinated Chicken

1/2 cup reduced-sodium
  chicken broth
1/2 cup dry white wine
3/4 cup sliced leeks
2 tablespoons lemon juice
1/2 teaspoon grated lemon
  rind
1/4 teaspoon allspice
4 chicken breast filets
1 cup plain nonfat or
  low-fat yogurt
1 tablespoon Dijon
  mustard
1 tablespoon chopped
  fresh parsley

- Combine chicken broth, wine, leeks, lemon juice, lemon rind and allspice in shallow dish. Rinse chicken and pat dry. Add to marinade. Marinate in refrigerator for 2 hours to overnight.
- Remove chicken from marinade, reserving marinade. Place chicken on rack in broiler pan. Broil for 8 to 12 minutes or until light brown. Remove to 8x10-inch baking dish.
- Bring reserved marinade to a boil in small saucepan; reduce heat. Simmer, covered, for 5 minutes. Cool for 10 minutes. Whisk in yogurt, mustard and parsley. Spoon over chicken.
- Bake at 350 degrees for 15 minutes or until chicken is tender. Serve over rice pilaf.
- Yield: 4 servings.

Prosciutini Chicken

6 chicken breast filets
Salt and pepper to taste
Flour
3 tablespoons butter
2 tablespoons olive oil
4 ounces thinly sliced
  prosciutini, or peppered
  ham
4 ounces shredded
  Fontina, Bel Paese or
  Edam cheese
4 teaspoons grated
  Parmesan cheese
1/4 cup chicken broth

- Slice each chicken filet horizontally into 2 pieces. Rinse and pat dry. Pound slightly to flatten on cutting board. Sprinkle lightly with salt and pepper; coat with flour.
- Brown chicken in mixture of butter and oil in heavy skillet over medium heat until golden brown; do not overcook. Remove to buttered shallow baking dish.
- Layer with prosciutini and shredded Fontina cheese; sprinkle with Parmesan cheese. Drizzle with chicken stock. Bake at 350 degrees for 10 minutes or until cheese melts.
- May prepare in advance, chill in refrigerator and bake for 20 minutes.
- Yield: 4 servings.

Polynesian Chicken

1 cup white cooking wine
1 (12-ounce) can
  pineapple juice
1 small onion, minced
1 teaspoon soy sauce
1 teaspoon Worcestershire
  sauce
1 clove of garlic, minced
Salt and pepper to taste
8 chicken breast filets

- Combine wine, pineapple juice, onion, soy sauce, Worcestershire sauce, garlic, salt and pepper in bowl; mix well.
- Rinse chicken and pat dry. Add to marinade. Marinate for 1 hour to overnight. Drain, reserving marinade.
- Place on rack in broiler pan. Broil for 10 to 15 minutes on each side or until tender, basting frequently with marinade.
- Yield: 4 to 6 servings.

Roman Grilled Chicken

4 chicken breast filets
1/4 cup olive oil and
  balsamic vinegar
  vinaigrette
1 tablespoon olive oil
1 1/2 teaspoons minced
  garlic
1 1/2 teaspoons Italian
  seasoning
1/4 teaspoon hot red
  pepper flakes
Salt and pepper to taste

- Rinse chicken and pat dry. Combine with vinaigrette, olive oil, garlic, Italian seasoning, pepper flakes, salt and pepper in plastic bag; mix to coat well.
- Marinate in refrigerator for 1 hour or longer; drain.
- Place on oiled grill or rack in broiler pan. Grill or broil 6 to 8 inches from heat source for 6 to 10 minutes on each side or until cooked through.
- Yield: 4 servings.

Sesame Chicken with Acorn Squash

2 tablespoons sesame oil
1 (1-inch) piece of ginger,
  peeled, sliced
3 cloves of garlic, chopped
Dried chili pepper to taste
1 teaspoon chili powder
1/2 cup white wine
1/4 cup soy sauce
4 chicken breast filets, cut
  into 3/4-inch strips
2 acorn squash
1/2 cup flour
2 tablespoons each black
  and white sesame seeds
3 tablespoons unsalted
  butter
3 carrots, peeled, sliced,
  blanched
20 snow peas, blanched
Flowerets of 1 small stalk
  broccoli

- Combine sesame oil, ginger, garlic, chili pepper, chili powder, wine and soy sauce in bowl; mix well. Rinse chicken and pat dry. Add to marinade. Marinate for 30 minutes to overnight.
- Cut squash into halves lengthwise. Place cut side down in baking dish; add 1/2 inch water. Bake at 350 degrees for 30 to 40 minutes or until tender or microwave on High for 15 minutes.
- Drain chicken, reserving 1/4 cup marinade. Coat chicken in mixture of flour and sesame seeds. Sauté in butter in skillet until golden brown. Remove chicken to bowl; drain skillet.
- Strain reserved marinade into skillet, stirring to deglaze. Add carrots, snow peas and broccoli. Cook until vegetables are heated through. Add chicken to vegetables; toss to coat well. Serve chicken and vegetables over squash.
- Yield: 4 servings.

Chicken Salsa

4 chicken breast filets
1/2 cup baking mix
1 tablespoon olive oil or
   peanut oil
1 (6-ounce) jar salsa
8 ounces part-skim
   mozzarella cheese,
   shredded
4 cups cooked rice

- Rinse chicken and pat dry; cut into strips. Shake with baking mix in small bag. Brown in heated olive oil in large skillet for 3 to 5 minutes.
- Remove chicken to 2-quart baking dish. Top with salsa and cheese. Bake at 375 degrees for 5 minutes or until cheese melts. Serve over rice.
- Yield: 2 to 4 servings.

Boneless Chicken with Ginger

1 pound boned chicken
   thighs
1 large onion, cut into
   wedges
2 tablespoons oil
6 large cloves of garlic,
   thinly sliced
1 tablespoon thinly
   shredded gingerroot
2 tablespoons honey
2 tablespoons Vietnamese
   fish sauce
2 tablespoons soy sauce
1/2 teaspoon five-spice
   powder
Freshly ground pepper to
   taste

- Cut chicken into 2-inch pieces; rinse and pat dry.
- Stir-fry onion in heated oil in wok or skillet over high heat until light brown.
- Add chicken. Stir-fry until golden brown. Add garlic, gingerroot, honey, fish sauce, soy sauce and five-spice powder, tossing to coat well.
- Cook for 3 minutes or until chicken is glazed; remove to hot platter. Sprinkle with pepper. Garnish with coriander sprigs. Serve with rice.
- May substitute duck, pork or fresh prawns for chicken.
- Yield: 4 servings.

Stir orange juice and a little peanut butter into skimmed
juices from roast chicken for a delicious gravy.

Stuffed Chicken Thighs

1/2 cup finely chopped celery
1/2 cup finely chopped onion
2 tablespoons bacon drippings
2 tablespoons dry sherry
1/4 teaspoon poultry seasoning
1/8 teaspoon pepper
2 cups soft bread crumbs
3 slices bacon, crisp-fried, crumbled
8 chicken thighs with skin, boned
1 tablespoon bacon drippings
1/2 teaspoon garlic salt
1/8 teaspoon pepper

- Sauté celery and onion in 2 tablespoons bacon drippings in skillet over medium heat for 4 minutes or until tender; remove from heat. Stir in wine, poultry seasoning and 1/8 teaspoon pepper. Add bread crumbs and bacon; mix well.
- Rinse chicken and pat dry. Place skin side on work surface. Spread each piece with crumb mixture. Roll up to enclose filling; secure with wooden picks.
- Place seam side down in shallow baking dish; brush with 1 tablespoon bacon drippings; sprinkle with garlic salt and 1/8 teaspoon pepper.
- Bake at 450 degrees for 7 minutes. Reduce oven temperature to 350 degrees. Bake for 45 minutes longer.
- Yield: 4 servings.

Chicken and Sausage Turnovers

8 chicken thighs
1/4 cup oil
1/2 cup chicken stock
8 pork sausage links, cooked
1/4 cup flour
1/2 teaspoon salt
2 cups milk
1 recipe 2-crust pie pastry

- Rinse chicken and pat dry. Brown in oil in skillet. Add chicken stock. Simmer, covered, for 20 minutes. Cool thighs. Remove bone carefully from each chicken thigh, leaving meat intact. Insert 1 sausage link in opening in each thigh.
- Blend flour and salt into drippings. Stir in milk. Cook over medium heat until thickened, stirring constantly. Cool.
- Cut pastry into eight 7-inch circles. Place 1 thigh on each circle; add 2 tablespoons cooled gravy. Moisten pastry; fold over to enclose filling and seal. Place on baking sheet. Bake at 375 degrees for 30 minutes or until golden brown. Serve hot with heated remaining gravy.
- Yield: 8 servings.

Chicken Crêpes Parisienne

3 eggs
2/3 cup flour
1 cup milk
1/2 teaspoon salt
2 cups sliced mushrooms
1/4 cup green onions
1/4 cup butter
3 tablespoons flour
1/2 teaspoon salt
Pepper to taste
1 cup milk
2 1/2 cups shredded
   Cheddar cheese
1 1/2 cups chopped cooked
   chicken

- Beat first 4 ingredients in bowl. Let stand for 30 minutes. Pour 1/4 cup batter at a time into hot, lightly greased 8-inch skillet. Cook just until light brown on bottom.
- Sauté mushrooms and green onions in butter in skillet. Stir in 3 tablespoons flour, 1/2 teaspoon salt and pepper. Add 1 cup milk gradually. Cook until thickened, stirring constantly. Stir in 1 1/2 cups cheese. Add chicken. Roll up 1/4 cup chicken mixture in each crêpe; place seam side down in 8x12-inch baking dish.
- Bake at 350 degrees for 20 minutes. Sprinkle with remaining 1 cup cheese. Bake just until cheese melts.
- Yield: 4 servings.

Chicken in Potato Boats

2 cups chopped cooked
   chicken
1 stalk celery, sliced
1/4 cup black olive halves
1 tablespoon chopped
   pimento
1/4 cup sour cream
1/2 teaspoon chili powder
1 (10-ounce) can cream of
   chicken soup
1/2 cup instant potato
   flakes
3 tablespoons butter
8 servings instant potato
   flakes
1 egg, slightly beaten
1/4 cup Parmesan cheese
3/4 cup sour cream
1/4 teaspoon salt

- Combine chicken, celery, olives, pimento, 1/4 cup sour cream, chili powder and half the soup in bowl; mix well.
- Sauté 1/2 cup instant potato flakes in butter until golden brown; set aside.
- Prepare the 8 servings of instant potato flakes using package directions, reducing water to 2 cups. Stir in egg and cheese. Spoon into 8 mounds on greased baking sheet; press with back of spoon to make indentation in each mound.
- Spoon chicken mixture into indentations; sprinkle with sautéed potatoes. Bake at 350 degrees for 30 minutes.
- Mix remaining soup with 3/4 cup sour cream and salt in saucepan. Cook until heated through. Serve over potato boats.
- Yield: 8 servings.

Roast Duck

1 (3 to 5-pound) duck
1 clove of garlic, cut into halves
Salt and pepper to taste
1 small onion, sliced
1 bay leaf
1/4 teaspoon ginger
1/4 teaspoon thyme
3 stalks celery, sliced
1 cup red currant jelly
1/2 cup red cooking wine
1 teaspoon ginger
Juice and grated rind of 1/2 orange
Juice of 1/2 lemon
2 teaspoons cornstarch

- Rinse duck inside and out; discard fat. Rub with garlic; sprinkle with salt and pepper.
- Combine onion, bay leaf, 1/4 teaspoon ginger, thyme and celery in bowl. Stuff into duck. Place in roasting pan.
- Combine remaining ingredients in saucepan. Simmer for 5 minutes, stirring constantly. Brush over duck.
- Place duck in 450-degree oven; reduce oven temperature to 350 degrees. Bake for 20 minutes per pound, basting with sauce every 20 minutes and turning and draining duck after 30 minutes.
- Yield: 2 servings.

Pheasant Fricassee

1 onion
4 cloves
2 (13-ounce) cans chicken broth
1 small carrot, chopped
1 tablespoon chopped chives
2 tablespoons chopped parsley
1 teaspoon salt
1/2 bay leaf
1 teaspoon parsley
3 peppercorns
2 or 3 pheasants, cut up
6 tablespoons flour
6 tablespoons oil
12 small white onions
1/2 teaspoon rosemary
1/2 teaspoon marjoram
3 tablespoons light cream
1 teaspoon lemon juice

- Stud onion with cloves. Combine with broth and next 7 ingredients in heavy saucepan. Bring to a boil; reduce heat.
- Rinse pheasant and pat dry. Coat with 3 tablespoons flour. Brown in 3 tablespoons oil in skillet.
- Add pheasant and small onions to saucepan. Simmer for 30 to 45 minutes or until tender. Remove pheasant and onions to baking dish, reserving stock.
- Stir 3 tablespoons flour into 3 tablespoons oil in skillet. Strain stock into skillet. Cook until smooth, whisking constantly. Add remaining ingredients. Cook until thickened, stirring constantly. Spoon over pheasant.
- Bake at 350 degrees until heated through, stirring constantly. Serve with mixture of white rice and brown rice.
- Yield: 6 servings.

SEAFOOD

CLASSIC CONNECTICUT CUISINE

MYSTIC SEAPORT • MYSTIC

Easter Seals
®

Bass in Beer Sauce

2 large onions, minced
1/4 cup butter
2 tablespoons flour
1 (12-ounce) bottle of beer
2 tablespoons brown sugar
1 teaspoon Worcestershire
  sauce
1 teaspoon salt
1/2 teaspoon pepper
3 pounds bass, cut into
  serving pieces

- Sauté onions in butter in large skillet until golden brown. Stir in flour. Cook for 2 minutes, stirring constantly.
- Add beer, brown sugar, Worcestershire sauce, salt and pepper. Cook until thickened, stirring constantly.
- Add fish. Cook until fish flakes easily. Remove fish to serving plate; spoon beer sauce over fish.
- Garnish with parsley sprigs.
- Yield: 6 servings.

Fish Fillets with Mustard Butter

2 pounds fresh or thawed
  frozen bluefish or other
  fish fillets
3/4 cup lemon juice
3 cups water
6 tablespoons butter
4 teaspoons prepared
  mustard
1/2 teaspoon paprika
3/4 teaspoon salt

- Cut fish fillets into serving pieces; arrange in single layer in 8x12-inch baking dish. Pour mixture of 3/4 cup lemon juice and water over fish.
- Marinate in refrigerator for 25 to 30 minutes; drain. Arrange in single layer on greased rack of broiler pan.
- Combine butter, 3 tablespoons lemon juice, mustard, paprika and salt in bowl; mix well. Brush over fish.
- Broil 4 inches from heat source for 4 to 6 minutes. Turn fish over and baste with butter mixture. Broil for 4 to 6 minutes longer or until fish flakes easily.
- Garnish with parsley. Serve with heated remaining butter.
- Yield: 6 servings.

Baked Flounder and Crab

2 pounds flounder or cod
1 pound crab meat
1/2 cup flour
5 tablespoons melted
  low-fat margarine
2 cups skim milk
1 teaspoon prepared
  mustard
Juice of 1/2 lemon
1 tablespoon chopped
  parsley
1 teaspoon salt
1/2 cup dry sherry
Buttered bread crumbs

- Cut fish into bite-sized pieces. Combine with crab meat in greased baking dish.
- Blend flour into melted margarine in saucepan. Cook for several minutes. Add milk. Cook until thickened, stirring constantly. Stir in mustard, lemon juice, parsley, salt and wine. Pour over fish.
- Top with buttered bread crumbs. Bake at 350 degrees for 1 hour.
- This recipe is from Connecticut State Senator Amelia P. Mustone.
- Yield: 8 servings.

Halibut Plaki

2 to 2 1/2 pounds (1-inch
  thick) halibut, cod or
  gray mullet
1/4 cup olive oil
2 large onions, thinly
  sliced
4 cloves of garlic
1 (16-ounce) can Italian
  plum tomatoes
Juice of 1/2 lemon
1 large bunch parsley,
  chopped
2 bay leaves
Rosemary, thyme, salt and
  pepper to taste

- Sauté fish briefly on both sides in olive oil in heavy skillet. Arrange in single layer in baking dish.
- Add onions and garlic to drippings in skillet. Sauté for 10 minutes or until tender. Add tomatoes, lemon juice, parsley, bay leaves, rosemary, thyme, salt and pepper; mix well. Simmer for 10 minutes, adding water or white wine if necessary for desired consistency. Pour over fish.
- Bake at 425 degrees for 5 minutes; cover with foil. Bake for 5 to 7 minutes longer or until fish flakes easily; discard bay leaves. Garnish with lemon wedges.
- Yield: 4 servings.

Crouton and Halibut Bake

1/2 cup mayonnaise
2 tablespoons lemon juice
1 egg, beaten
2 cups seasoned croutons
1 cup whole kernel corn
  with sweet peppers,
  drained
1 medium tomato, chopped
1/4 cup shredded Swiss or
  Cheddar cheese
2 tablespoons minced
  onion
2 pounds frozen skinned
  halibut, pollack,
  flounder or sole fillets,
  thawed
1 teaspoon salt

- Combine mayonnaise, lemon juice and egg in bowl. Stir in croutons, corn, tomato, cheese and onion. Spread 2 cups of the mixture in 8x12-inch baking dish.
- Sprinkle halibut with salt; arrange in prepared dish. Top with remaining crouton mixture.
- Bake at 350 degrees for 45 to 50 minutes or until fish flakes easily. Garnish with lemon wedges.
- Yield: 6 servings.

Salmon with Artichoke Court Bouillon

1 cup white wine
4 cups water
Juice of 1 lemon
1 onion, sliced
12 ounces baby carrots,
  peeled
2 bay leaves
2 cups undrained canned
  artichoke hearts
6 (6-ounce) salmon fillets
Salt and pepper to taste
1 cup water
1 cup butter, cut into
  1-inch cubes
24 cherry tomatoes, cut
  into quarters
1/4 cup chopped chives
2 tablespoons chopped dill

- Combine wine, 4 cups water, lemon juice, onion, carrots and bay leaves in saucepan. Bring to a boil over high heat. Boil for 5 to 7 minutes or until carrots are tender-crisp.
- Drain artichoke hearts, reserving 1/2 cup liquid. Add artichoke hearts to saucepan. Cook for 1 minute longer. Chill in refrigerator.
- Season fish with salt and pepper. Steam in 1 cup water and reserved artichoke liquid in saucepan until salmon flakes easily but is still firm.
- Reheat artichoke heart mixture. Add butter, tomatoes, chives, dill, salt and pepper; discard bay leaves. Ladle into soup bowls. Top with salmon; garnish with additional dill and chives.
- Yield: 6 servings.

Salmon Corn Cakes

3 eggs
2 tablespoons flour
2 teaspoons lemon juice
2 drops of red pepper
   sauce
1 teaspoon salt
Pepper to taste
1 (12-ounce) can whole
   kernel corn, drained
1 (7-ounce) can salmon,
   drained, flaked
1/2 cup sour cream
1/4 cup shredded
   American cheese
2 tablespoons chopped
   pimento

- Combine eggs, flour, lemon juice, pepper sauce, salt and pepper in bowl; beat with rotary beater until foamy. Stir in corn and salmon.
- Drop by generous 1/4 cupfuls onto hot greased griddle; press lightly to flatten. Bake for 3 minutes on each side or until golden brown.
- Combine sour cream, cheese and pimento in saucepan. Cook just until bubbly over low heat, stirring constantly. Serve with salmon corn cakes.
- Yield: 4 servings.

Salmon in Dill and Caper Sauce

1 (1 1/2-pound) salmon
   fillet
1 cup mayonnaise or
   reduced-calorie
   mayonnaise
1/2 cup white wine
2 tablespoons dill
2 tablespoons capers

- Rinse fish and pat dry; place in rectangular baking dish.
- Combine mayonnaise, wine, dill and capers in bowl; mix well. Spread over salmon.
- Microwave on High for 10 minutes or until fish flakes easily, turning once or twice.
- May bake in 375-degree oven for 20 minutes or vary seasonings if preferred.
- Yield: 3 to 4 servings.

Make a delicious **Kiwi Sauce for Fish** by processing 2 green bell peppers, 1/2 jalapeño pepper, 1 onion, 4 kiwifruit and juice of half a lemon in a blender until smooth. Then combine with 1/4 cup water, 1/4 cup white wine and cumin, salt and pepper to taste in a saucepan and heat to serving temperature. The sauce is especially good with mahi-mahi.

Grilled Salmon Steaks

1 ounce sun-dried
   tomatoes
1 cup water
1/2 teaspoon minced garlic
2 tablespoons catsup
2 tablespoons tomato paste
2 tablespoons balsamic
   vinegar
2 tablespoons cider vinegar
2 tablespoons fresh lemon
   juice
1/2 cup water
1/4 cup oil
1 1/2 teaspoons minced
   fresh parsley
1 1/2 teaspoons minced
   drained capers
1 tablespoon minced fresh
   chives
1/2 teaspoon dried
   tarragon, crumbled
1/4 teaspoon salt
1/2 teaspoon freshly
   ground black pepper
1/8 teaspoon cayenne
   pepper
1/2 cup water
4 (8-ounce) salmon
   steaks, 1 inch thick

- Simmer tomatoes in 1 cup water in small saucepan for 3 minutes; cool to room temperature. Drain and chop tomatoes, reserving cooking liquid.
- Combine reserved liquid, tomatoes, garlic, catsup, tomato paste, vinegars, lemon juice, 1/2 cup water, oil, parsley, capers, chives, tarragon, salt, black pepper and cayenne pepper in bowl; mix well. Let stand, covered, for 2 to 12 hours.
- Combine tomato mixture with 1/2 cup water in shallow glass dish. Add salmon steaks, turning to coat well. Marinate in refrigerator for 2 hours. Drain, reserving marinade.
- Grill or broil salmon 4 inches from heat source for 13 to 15 minutes or just until cooked through, brushing with reserved marinade.
- Heat remaining marinade in small saucepan. Serve with salmon.
- Do not use oil-pack sun-dried tomatoes in this recipe.
- Yield: 4 servings.

Marinated Swordfish

1 pound swordfish, 1 inch
   thick
1/2 cup dry white wine
2 tablespoons Dijon
   mustard
2 tablespoons lemon juice
1/4 teaspoon pepper

- Marinate swordfish in mixture of wine, mustard, lemon juice and pepper in 9x13-inch dish in refrigerator for 1 hour or longer; drain.
- Place fish on rack in broiler pan. Broil for 6 minutes on each side.
- Yield: 2 servings.

Scrod Oreganato

6 clams
6 mussels
1 pound scrod
Flour
6 tablespoons olive oil
2 cloves of garlic, minced
1 tablespoon chopped
  parsley
2/3 teaspoon oregano
1 teaspoon basil
1/2 cup white wine
6 tablespoons butter
1 cup clam juice
1 teaspoon each salt and
  pepper
8 ounces uncooked
  linguine

- Scrub clams and mussels with stiff brush; rinse in cold water.
- Coat fish with flour. Brown on both sides in hot olive oil in skillet.
- Add clams, mussels, garlic, parsley, oregano and basil; remove from heat. Stir in wine, butter, clam juice, salt and pepper.
- Simmer, covered, just until seafood is cooked through; do not boil.
- Cook pasta *al dente* using package directions; drain. Spoon seafood over pasta to serve.
- Yield: 2 servings.

Broccoli and Sole au Gratin

1/4 cup flour
3/4 teaspoon salt
1/4 cup melted butter
11/2 cups milk
1 cup shredded Swiss
  cheese
1 pound fish fillets
1 tablespoon lemon juice
1/2 teaspoon garlic salt
1/4 teaspoon pepper
Paprika to taste
2 cups thawed frozen
  chopped broccoli

- Whisk flour and salt into melted butter in saucepan over medium heat. Cook until bubbly. Stir in milk gradually. Cook for 1 minute or until thickened, stirring constantly. Reduce heat. Stir in cheese until melted.
- Cut fish crosswise into 4 pieces; place in center of 8x12-inch baking dish. Sprinkle with lemon juice, garlic salt and pepper. Spoon half the sauce over fish; sprinkle with paprika.
- Fold broccoli into remaining sauce. Spoon around fish. Bake at 375 degrees for 35 to 40 minutes or until fish flakes easily.
- Yield: 2 to 3 servings.

Sole Fillets with Butter Sauce

1/4 cup butter
1/4 cup white wine or
    apple juice
2 bay leaves
1 teaspoon rosemary
1 teaspoon oregano
1/2 teaspoon garlic powder
1/2 teaspoon salt
1/8 teaspoon pepper
1 pound frozen sole
    fillets, thawed, drained

- Melt butter in heavy 12-inch skillet over medium-low heat. Add wine, bay leaves, rosemary, oregano, garlic powder, salt and pepper; mix well.
- Add fish to skillet. Simmer, covered, for 10 to 15 minutes or until fish flakes easily. Remove fish to warm platter; increase heat to high.
- Bring sauce to a boil. Cook for 1 to 2 minutes or until slightly thickened; discard bay leaves. Spoon over fish to serve.
- Yield: 4 servings.

Barbecued Swordfish Kabobs

1/2 cup olive oil
Juice of 1 lemon
1 tablespoon Dijon
    mustard
1 clove of garlic, minced
1 tablespoon minced
    fresh dill
3 1/2 pounds swordfish
    steaks, 1 to 1 1/2 inches
    thick
Cherry tomatoes
2 small zucchini, sliced
    1/2-inch thick

- Whisk olive oil, lemon juice, mustard, garlic and dill together in shallow dish.
- Cut swordfish into cubes. Add to marinade. Marinate in refrigerator for 2 hours to overnight. Drain, reserving marinade.
- Thread fish, tomatoes and zucchini alternately onto skewers. Brush with reserved marinade.
- Grill until swordfish is cooked through, brushing occasionally with marinade.
- Yield: 8 servings.

Cook fish for 10 minutes for each inch of thickness. This time applies to steaks, fillets or whole fish and to all cooking methods.

Clam Pizzas

4¼ cups flour
2 packages fast-rising
  yeast
1 teaspoon sugar
2 teaspoons salt
2 tablespoons olive oil
1¾ cups water
2 tablespoons olive oil
1 teaspoon each tarragon,
  oregano, basil and
  rosemary
½ teaspoon each salt and
  pepper
2 slices bacon, chopped,
  partially cooked
5 cloves of garlic, chopped
1 small yellow onion,
  chopped
1 large tomato, thinly
  sliced, seeded
1 (10-ounce) can minced
  clams, drained
1½ cups shredded low-fat
  skim milk mozzarella
  cheese

- Mix 3 cups flour, yeast, sugar and 2 teaspoons salt in large mixer bowl.
- Heat 2 tablespoons olive oil and water to 125 degrees in saucepan. Add to flour mixture gradually, beating to mix well.
- Add enough remaining flour to form dough. Knead on floured surface for 8 to 10 minutes or until smooth and elastic. Cover with plastic wrap. Let rise for 10 minutes.
- Press dough into two 12-inch pizza pans sprayed with nonstick cooking spray.
- Spread each with 1 tablespoon olive oil; sprinkle with mixture of tarragon, oregano, basil, rosemary and ½ teaspoon salt and pepper. Layer with bacon, garlic, onion, tomato, clams and cheese.
- Bake at 500 degrees on lowest oven rack for 12 to 14 minutes or until bubbly and golden brown.
- Yield: 8 servings.

Crab Imperial

1 pound crab meat
½ cup (or less)
  mayonnaise
1 to 2 tablespoons capers
½ teaspoon (or less) salt
⅛ teaspoon pepper
½ cup dry bread crumbs
Paprika to taste

- Combine crab meat, mayonnaise, capers, salt and pepper in bowl; mix well. Spoon into baking shells; sprinkle with bread crumbs and paprika.
- Bake at 350 degrees for 25 minutes.
- May add 1 clove of garlic sautéed in 1 tablespoon butter and Microwave on Medium for 4 minutes if preferred.
- Yield: 4 servings.

Crab Cakes

2 (7-ounce) cans crab
  meat, drained, flaked
2 slices bread, torn into
  1/4-inch pieces
1/2 cup baking mix
1/2 cup mayonnaise or
  mayonnaise-type salad
  dressing
1 egg
1/2 teaspoon
  Worcestershire sauce
1/8 teaspoon paprika
Nutmeg to taste
1/4 teaspoon salt
1/3 cup baking mix
2 tablespoons butter

- Combine crab meat, bread, 1/2 cup baking mix, mayonnaise, egg, Worcestershire sauce, paprika, nutmeg and salt in bowl; mix well.
- Drop by 1/3 cupfuls into 1/3 cup baking mix, turning to coat well. Shape into 2 1/2 to 3-inch patties.
- Brown in heated butter in 10-inch skillet for 10 to 15 minutes or until brown on both sides. Serve with chili sauce or tartar sauce.
- Yield: 8 servings.

Crab Foo Yung

4 eggs, beaten
7 ounces fresh bean
  sprouts, rinsed, drained
1/3 cup thinly sliced green
  onions
1 cup flaked cooked crab
  meat
1/8 teaspoon garlic powder
1/2 teaspoon salt
1/8 teaspoon pepper
2 tablespoons oil
1 chicken bouillon cube
1/2 cup water
1 teaspoon cornstarch
1 teaspoon sugar
2 teaspoons soy sauce
1 teaspoon vinegar

- Combine eggs, bean sprouts, green onions, crab meat, garlic powder, salt and pepper in bowl; mix well.
- Heat just enough oil in skillet to cover bottom of pan. Spoon about 1/4 cup crab meat mixture into oil as for pancakes. Bake until set and light brown, turning once; remove to warm platter. Repeat with remaining batter, adding oil as needed.
- Dissolve chicken bouillon cube in 1/2 cup water in saucepan. Add cornstarch, sugar, soy sauce and vinegar; blend well. Cook until thickened, stirring constantly. Serve with crab pancakes.
- Yield: 5 servings.

Bud's Lobster Newburg

12 to 14 ounces fresh or
    frozen lobster meat
2 tablespoons butter
4 cups milk or skim milk
6 tablespoons butter
1/2 cup flour
1 tablespoon
    Worcestershire sauce
2 dashes Tabasco sauce
1 to 2 teaspoons paprika
2 to 3 tablespoons sherry
8 slices bread, toasted,
    sliced diagonally

- Sauté lobster lightly in 2 tablespoons butter in large skillet; remove lobster to bowl. Chill in refrigerator.
- Drain juices from lobster into milk in glass measure. Microwave until warm.
- Melt 6 tablespoons butter in skillet. Whisk in flour. Stir in milk mixture gradually. Cook until thickened, stirring constantly.
- Stir in Worcestershire sauce, Tabasco sauce and paprika. Add lobster and wine. Cook until heated through. Serve on toast points.
- Yield: 4 servings.

Lobster Newburg

4 pounds lobster tails
Salt to taste
1/3 cup butter
Cayenne pepper to taste
1/3 cup sherry
2 cups cream
4 egg yolks
2 tablespoons Cognac

- Cook lobster tails in salted water in saucepan for 12 minutes; drain. Cut off underside of shell and remove meat in 1 piece. Slice 1/2 inch thick.
- Sauté lobster meat lightly in 1/4 cup of the butter in skillet. Sprinkle with cayenne pepper; add wine. Cook until wine is slightly reduced.
- Reduce heat to low. Stir in mixture of cream and egg yolks. Cook until thickened, stirring constantly.
- Stir in remaining butter and Cognac. Cook until heated through; adjust seasonings. Serve over rice or buttered toast points.
- Yield: 4 servings.

Lobster Tails with Macadamia Butter

4 lobster tails
Salt to taste
2 tablespoons melted
  butter
1/4 cup melted butter
1/4 cup chopped
  macadamia nuts

- Cut lobster tails into halves lengthwise. Simmer in salted water in saucepan for 6 minutes; drain.
- Arrange on baking sheet; brush with 2 tablespoons melted butter. Broil for 4 to 5 minutes or just until light brown.
- Heat 1/4 cup butter in saucepan until it begins to brown. Add macadamia nuts. Cook for 1 minute. Place lobster tails on serving plates; spoon macadamia butter over top.
- Yield: 4 servings.

Oyster Stew

4 large potatoes, peeled,
  chopped
2 medium onions, chopped
1/2 cup milk
1 cup chopped celery
Salt to taste
8 slices bacon, cut into
  1/4-inch pieces
2 medium onions, chopped
2 tablespoons butter
1 cup milk
1/2 cup heavy cream
1 pint shucked oysters
  with liquid
Chopped parsley to taste
Salt and pepper to taste
1 tablespoon butter
Paprika to taste

- Combine potatoes and 2 onions with water to cover in saucepan. Cook until tender; drain. Process half the mixture with 1/2 cup milk in food processor.
- Cook celery in salted water in saucepan until tender; drain. Cook bacon in skillet until crisp; remove with slotted spoon. Add 2 onions to drippings in skillet. Sauté until golden brown.
- Melt 2 tablespoons butter in double boiler. Stir in 1 cup milk and cream. Add puréed vegetables. Cook until heated through.
- Stir in undrained oysters. Cook for 5 minutes or until edges of oysters curl. Add bacon, onion mixture, remaining potatoes and onions, celery, parsley, salt and pepper; mix well. Cook until heated through.
- Ladle into soup bowls. Top with butter and paprika. Flavor improves if made a day in advance and reheated.
- Yield: 2 to 3 servings.

Scallops Broiled in Garlic Butter

2 large cloves of garlic,
  cut into halves
1 cup butter
Chopped onion to taste
2 tablespoons chopped
  parsley
1/2 teaspoon tarragon
1/2 teaspoon salt
1/4 teaspoon pepper
2 pounds scallops

- Brown garlic in butter in saucepan; remove with slotted spoon and discard. Add onion, parsley, tarragon, salt and pepper; mix well.
- Rinse and drain scallops; place in shallow baking dish. Drizzle with seasoned butter.
- Broil for 3 minutes on each side or until cooked through. May move closer to heat source during last minute of cooking time to brown if desired.
- Yield: 6 servings.

Scallops and Fish Casserole

1/2 green bell pepper,
  chopped
1 small onion, chopped
2 stalks celery, chopped
Butter
8 ounces haddock fillets
8 ounces sea scallops
1 can frozen shrimp soup,
  thawed
1 small can pimento
1 small can evaporated
  milk
Seasonings to taste
Buttered crumbs

- Sauté green pepper, onion and celery in butter in saucepan until tender.
- Cut fish into 3 or 4 small pieces. Arrange on top of vegetables. Simmer, covered, for 5 minutes.
- Cut scallops into 2 or 3 pieces. Add to saucepan. Cook for 5 minutes. Stir in soup, pimento, evaporated milk and seasonings.
- Spoon into greased baking dish. Cool to room temperature. Chill, covered, overnight.
- Sprinkle with buttered crumbs. Bake at 350 degrees for 30 to 40 minutes or until heated through.
- Yield: 6 servings.

Add exciting new flavor to poached, broiled or sautéed
fish by adding a dash of grated or ground ginger.

Scallop Stew

5 tablespoons butter
1/4 teaspoon
   Worcestershire sauce
1/4 teaspoon celery salt
8 ounces scallops
1 1/2 cups light cream
Salt and pepper to taste
2 pats butter

- Melt 5 tablespoons butter in saucepan. Stir in Worcestershire sauce and celery salt. Cook for several minutes.
- Add scallops. Cook for 2 minutes, stirring frequently. Stir in cream.
- Bring to a simmer. Season to taste. Ladle into soup bowls. Top servings with pat of butter.
- May use sea scallops and cut into quarters.
- Yield: 2 servings.

Paella

8 ounces chicken legs
8 ounces chicken thighs
1/4 cup (or more) olive oil
Chopped garlic to taste
2 large onions, chopped
1/2 cup white cooking wine
1 large can chicken broth
2 tablespoons paprika
1/4 cup bay leaves
16 ounces linguica,
   chopped
2 cups sliced mushrooms
2 cups uncooked rice
16 ounces peeled shrimp
16 ounces scallops
16 ounces clams

- Rinse chicken and pat dry. Brown in 1/4 cup olive oil in large saucepan; remove to bowl. Add additional olive oil if needed.
- Add garlic and onions to saucepan. Sauté until tender. Stir in wine. Cook until wine has nearly evaporated.
- Stir in chicken broth, paprika, bay leaves, sausage and mushrooms. Cook, covered, for 15 minutes.
- Add rice. Simmer for 10 minutes. Add shrimp, scallops and clams. Cook just until seafood is cooked through; discard bay leaves. Serve immediately.
- Yield: 5 or 6 servings.

After peeling shrimp, remove the odor from your hands by rubbing them with fresh parsley.

Charred Shrimp in Barbecue Sauce

1 teaspoon cornstarch
2 tablespoons sherry
3 tablespoons tomato
　sauce
2 tablespoons chicken
　stock
2 tablespoons dark brown
　sugar
4 teaspoons soy sauce
2 teaspoons wine vinegar
1 teaspoon hot sauce or
　hot oil
1 pound (21 to 25-count)
　medium shrimp
3 tablespoons peanut oil
2 teaspoons minced garlic
1/2 cup shredded scallions

- Blend first 8 ingredients in bowl; set aside.
- Cut shrimp shells along backs with scissors, cutting halfway into shrimp. Leave shrimp in shells; discard legs. Rinse in cold water; pat dry.
- Heat wok over high heat for 1 minute. Add 2½ tablespoons peanut oil. Heat until hot but not smoking. Add shrimp. Stir-fry for 4 minutes or until almost cooked and charred. Pour into heated dish.
- Add remaining ½ tablespoon peanut oil, garlic and scallions to wok. Stir-fry for 30 seconds. Add sauce. Stir-fry until thickened, stirring constantly. Add shrimp. Cook for 30 seconds. Serve immediately.
- Yield: 3 servings.

Shrimp Cantonese

1 (14-ounce) can
　pineapple chunks
1/4 cup sugar
2 tablespoons cornstarch
1/4 cup vinegar
2 teaspoons soy sauce
2 stalks celery, chopped
4 green onions, sliced
1/2 green bell pepper, cut
　into 1/4-inch strips
2 (4-ounce) cans jumbo
　shrimp, drained
1 tomato, cut into 8 wedges
1 cup rice, cooked
1½ cups shredded Swiss
　cheese
1/3 cup toasted sliced
　almonds

- Drain pineapple, reserving juice. Add enough water to reserved juice to measure 1 cup. Stir into mixture of sugar and cornstarch in saucepan. Add vinegar and soy sauce gradually.
- Cook over medium heat until thickened, stirring constantly. Cook for 1 minute longer, stirring constantly. Stir in pineapple, celery, green onions and green pepper.
- Add shrimp and tomato; mix gently. Cook until heated through.
- Combine hot rice with cheese in bowl. Pack into buttered 4-cup mold. Invert immediately onto serving tray. Top with shrimp mixture; sprinkle with almonds.
- Yield: 6 to 8 servings.

Shrimp with Braised Leeks

3 leek bulbs
2 cups chicken stock
Salt and pepper to taste
1½ pounds small shrimp,
  peeled, deveined
2 tablespoons butter
2 tablespoons olive oil
1 cup heavy cream
3 tablespoons minced
  parsley

- Cut leeks lengthwise into quarters; cut quarters into 1-inch pieces. Rinse well. Cook in chicken stock in saucepan over medium heat for 10 minutes or until tender; drain. Sprinkle leeks with salt and pepper; keep warm.
- Sauté shrimp in butter and olive oil in skillet over medium heat for 1 minute. Add cream and 2 tablespoons parsley. Cook for 1 minute longer or until shrimp are tender.
- Spoon leeks onto 6 serving plates. Remove shrimp from sauce with slotted spoon and place on leeks. Cover and keep warm.
- Cook sauce in saucepan over high heat until reduced by ⅓; season with salt and pepper. Spoon over shrimp; sprinkle with remaining 1 tablespoon parsley.
- Yield: 6 servings.

Ragin' Cajun Shrimp

4 cloves of garlic, chopped
½ teaspoon chopped
  shallots
3 tablespoons butter
2 tablespoons olive oil
12 medium shrimp,
  peeled, deveined
1 tablespoon sliced
  shallots
½ teaspoon Cajun spice
1 tablespoon vodka
½ lemon

- Sauté garlic and chopped shallots lightly in heated butter and olive oil in skillet over medium heat.
- Add shrimp and sliced shallots. Sauté until shrimp are tender. Add spice and vodka. Ignite vodka and allow flames to subside. Squeeze lemon juice over top.
- Yield: 2 to 4 servings.

Shrimp and Spaghetti

1 pound shrimp, cooked, peeled, cut into halves
1 pound feta cheese, crumbled
1/4 to 1/3 cup finely chopped scallions
1 can tomatoes, drained, chopped
1 1/2 teaspoons oregano
1 (1-pound) package spaghetti

- Combine shrimp, cheese, scallions, tomatoes and oregano in bowl; toss to mix well. Chill in refrigerator for several hours; let stand until room temperature.
- Cook pasta using package directions; drain. Combine with shrimp mixture in large bowl; toss gently to mix.
- Yield: 4 servings.

Scallops and Shrimp with Linguine

16 ounces fresh or thawed frozen sea scallops
8 ounces fresh or thawed frozen medium shrimp in shells
1/2 cup sliced green onions
3 cloves of garlic, minced
3 tablespoons olive oil or vegetable oil
3 tablespoons margarine or butter
2 teaspoons parsley flakes
1 teaspoon dried basil, crushed
1/4 teaspoon crushed red pepper
2 cups fresh or thawed frozen pea pods
1/4 cup oil-pack sun-dried tomatoes, drained, cut into thin strips
10 ounces linguine, cooked, drained
3 tablespoons grated Parmesan or Romano cheese

- Cut scallops into halves. Combine with shrimp in bowl.
- Sauté green onions and garlic in heated olive oil and margarine in skillet over medium heat for 30 seconds.
- Add half the shrimp and scallop mixture, parsley flakes, basil and red pepper. Sauté for 3 to 4 minutes or until seafood is cooked through. Remove with slotted spoon to bowl. Repeat with remaining shrimp and scallops. Return seafood to skillet with pea pods and sun-dried tomatoes. Sauté for 2 minutes.
- Combine seafood mixture with pasta in large bowl; toss to mix well. Spoon onto serving platter; sprinkle with cheese.
- Yield: 6 servings.

Texas Shrimp and Rice

3 tablespoons olive oil
2 cups chopped onions
1 cup chopped green bell
   pepper
2 tablespoons Seasoning
   Mix (below)
3 bay leaves
2 tablespoons fresh lemon
   juice
2 tablespoons fresh lime
   juice
1½ cups uncooked rice
1 (4-ounce) can chopped
   green chilies
1 tablespoon Seasoning
   Mix (below)
3 cups seafood stock or
   clam juice
½ teaspoon minced garlic
2¼ pounds large shrimp,
   peeled
1 tablespoon Seasoning
   Mix (below)
½ cup chopped fresh
   parsley
1 cup chopped green
   onions

- Heat olive oil in large heavy saucepan for 4 to 5 minutes or until very hot. Add onions, green pepper and 2 tablespoons Seasoning Mix. Sauté for 2 minutes. Add bay leaves. Sauté for 5 minutes.

- Add lemon juice, lime juice and rice. Sauté for 4 minutes or until rice is light brown. Stir in chilies and 1 tablespoon Seasoning Mix. Cook until mixture forms a light crust on bottom of saucepan.

- Add seafood stock, stirring to deglaze saucepan. Cook for 4 minutes, stirring occasionally. Add garlic. Cook for 1 minute. Add shrimp and 1 tablespoon Seasoning Mix; mix well.

- Cook, covered, for 2 minutes. Stir in parsley and green onions. Cook for 2 minutes longer. Let stand, covered, for 15 minutes before serving; discard bay leaves.

- Yield: 6 servings.

Prepare **Seasoning Mix** by mixing ¼ teaspoon each amcho chili powder and guajillo chili powder, 1 teaspoon each paprika, onion powder, garlic powder, sweet basil and white pepper, 1½ teaspoons each dried cilantro and ground cumin, 1¾ teaspoons dried oregano and ½ teaspoon cayenne pepper in a small bowl. Store unused mix in airtight container.

VEGETABLES &
SIDE DISHES

BARN WITH BOAT BUMPERS • SALEM

Asparagus Meringue

2 pounds asparagus,
  trimmed
Salt to taste
3/4 cup mayonnaise
1/4 cup sour cream
1 1/2 teaspoons Dijon
  mustard
1 teaspoon lemon juice
1 1/2 tablespoons minced
  chives
4 egg whites
1/2 teaspoon salt
1/4 teaspoon pepper
Sugar to taste

- Bring asparagus, salt to taste and enough water to cover to a boil in saucepan. Boil for 2 to 3 minutes or until tender-crisp; drain. Rinse with cold water. Drain and pat dry. Arrange in shallow baking dish. Place in warm oven.
- Combine mayonnaise, sour cream, Dijon mustard, lemon juice and chives in bowl; mix well.
- Beat egg whites with 1/2 teaspoon salt and pepper in mixer bowl until soft peaks form. Sprinkle with sugar. Beat until stiff peaks form. Fold into mayonnaise mixture. Spoon over asparagus. Broil for 3 minutes or until light brown.
- Yield: 4 servings.

Asparagus and Mushroom Casserole

4 cups mushroom halves
1 cup chopped onion
1/4 cup butter
2 teaspoons flour
1 teaspoon chicken
  bouillon granules
1/2 teaspoon salt
Pepper to taste
1/2 teaspoon nutmeg
1 cup milk
2 (10-ounce) packages
  frozen cut asparagus,
  cooked, drained
1/4 cup chopped pimentos
1/2 cup sliced water
  chestnuts
1 1/2 teaspoons lemon juice
3/4 cup soft bread crumbs
1 teaspoon melted butter

- Sauté mushrooms and onion in 1/4 cup butter in saucepan for 10 minutes or until tender. Remove vegetables to bowl.
- Stir flour, bouillon granules, salt, pepper and nutmeg into pan drippings. Add milk; mix well.
- Cook until bubbly, stirring constantly. Stir in sautéed vegetables, asparagus, pimentos, water chestnuts and lemon juice. Spoon into 1 1/2-quart baking dish. Sprinkle with bread crumbs; drizzle with 1 teaspoon melted butter.
- Bake at 350 degrees for 35 minutes.
- Yield: 8 to 10 servings.

Beets in Orange and Lemon Sauce

2 pounds beets
1/2 cup orange juice
1/2 cup lemon juice
2 tablespoons cider
  vinegar
1 1/2 tablespoons
  cornstarch
2 tablespoons sugar
1 teaspoon salt
1/4 cup butter
1 teaspoon grated orange
  rind
1 teaspoon grated lemon
  rind

- Bring beets and enough cold water to cover to a boil in saucepan; reduce heat.
- Simmer, covered, for 45 minutes or until tender; drain. Cool. Peel beets; cut into 1/4-inch slices.
- Bring orange juice, lemon juice, cider vinegar and cornstarch to a boil in same saucepan, stirring constantly. Boil until thickened, stirring constantly. Stir in sugar, salt and beets.
- Simmer for 10 minutes or until heated through, stirring occasionally. Stir in butter, orange rind and lemon rind.
- Yield: 4 to 6 servings.

Beets and Carrots

5 medium beets
2 medium carrots, cut
  into 1/4-inch slices
3 tablespoons butter
1 tablespoon dried chives
1/2 teaspoon salt
1/2 teaspoon dillweed
1/8 teaspoon pepper

- Bring beets and enough water to cover to a boil in saucepan; reduce heat.
- Cook, covered, over medium heat for 35 to 40 minutes or until beets are tender. Chop beets, discarding skin and root ends.
- Bring carrots and enough water to cover to a boil in saucepan; reduce heat.
- Cook, covered, over medium heat for 8 to 10 minutes or until tender; drain.
- Melt butter in saucepan. Stir in beets, carrots, chives, salt, dillweed and pepper.
- Cook over medium heat for 5 to 7 minutes or until heated through, stirring occasionally. Garnish with sour cream.
- Yield: 4 servings.

Corn-Stuffed Green Pepper Boats

2 quarts water
2 large green bell
  peppers, cut into halves
  lengthwise
3 tablespoons butter
1 cup cooked white rice
1 (8-ounce) can whole
  kernel corn, drained
1/2 teaspoon marjoram
1/2 teaspoon onion powder
1/4 teaspoon salt
1/8 teaspoon pepper
2 tablespoons chopped
  pimento

- Bring water to a boil in saucepan; reduce heat. Add green peppers.
- Simmer for 3 minutes; drain. Place green peppers cut side up in 8x8-inch baking dish.
- Melt butter in saucepan. Stir in rice, corn, marjoram, onion powder, salt, pepper and pimento.
- Fill green pepper halves with rice mixture.
- Bake at 350 degrees for 20 to 25 minutes or until heated through.
- Yield: 4 servings.

Lemon Broccoli Almondine

1/2 cup water
Salt to taste
12 ounces broccoli,
  trimmed, cut into spears
1/4 cup butter
1/4 cup sliced almonds,
  toasted
1/4 teaspoon salt
1 teaspoon lemon juice
1/4 teaspoon grated lemon
  rind

- Bring water and salt to a boil in saucepan; reduce heat. Add broccoli.
- Cook, covered, over medium heat for 10 minutes or until tender; drain.
- Melt butter in saucepan. Stir in almonds, salt, lemon juice and lemon rind.
- Cook over medium heat for 2 to 3 minutes or until heated through, stirring occasionally.
- Arrange broccoli on serving platter; drizzle with butter mixture.
- Yield: 4 servings.

Broccoli with Bleu Cheese

1 tablespoon butter
1 tablespoon flour
Salt to taste
1/2 cup milk
1/3 cup crumbled bleu
  cheese
2 teaspoons prepared
  mustard
1 (10-ounce) package
  frozen cut broccoli,
  cooked, drained

• Melt butter in saucepan. Stir in flour and salt. Add milk; mix well.
• Cook until bubbly, stirring constantly. Stir in bleu cheese and mustard. Add broccoli; mix well.
• Cook until heated through, stirring occasionally.
• Yield: 3 to 4 servings.

Broccoli Surprise

1 (14-ounce) jar artichoke
  hearts, sliced
1/2 cup melted butter
8 ounces cream cheese,
  softened
1 1/2 teaspoons lemon juice
1/2 teaspoon
  Worcestershire sauce
Garlic salt to taste
Tabasco sauce to taste
2 (10-ounce) packages
  frozen chopped
  broccoli, cooked,
  drained
Bread crumbs

• Arrange artichokes in 1 1/2-quart baking dish.
• Combine butter, cream cheese and lemon juice in bowl; mix well. Stir in Worcestershire sauce, garlic salt and Tabasco sauce. Add broccoli; mix well. Spoon over artichokes; sprinkle with bread crumbs.
• Bake at 350 degrees for 25 minutes.
• Yield: 6 to 8 servings.

Brussels Sprouts with Sour Cream

1¹/2 pounds Brussels
  sprouts
1 bunch scallions with
  tops
8 ounces small mushrooms
2 tablespoons butter
¹/2 cup white cooking wine
2 cups sour cream
Salt and pepper to taste
8 ounces Swiss cheese,
  shredded

- Steam Brussels sprouts in steamer for 10 minutes or until tender. Arrange in baking dish.
- Chop scallions and tops, reserving tops for garnish.
- Sauté scallions and mushrooms in butter in saucepan. Add white wine; mix well. Stir in sour cream gradually. Season with salt and pepper.
- Cook over medium heat until heated through, stirring constantly; do not boil. Spoon over Brussels sprouts; sprinkle with cheese.
- Bake at 450 degrees for 5 minutes or until cheese melts. Garnish with reserved chopped scallion tops.
- Yield: 4 servings.

Brussels Sprouts with Yogurt

1 tablespoon butter
2 pounds Brussels sprouts
Salt to taste
2 small tomatoes, chopped
2 teaspoons chopped
  chives
¹/2 teaspoon nutmeg
Salt and pepper to taste
1 cup plain yogurt
¹/4 cup grated Parmesan
  cheese
¹/4 cup slivered almonds,
  toasted

- Spread butter in baking dish.
- Bring Brussels sprouts, salt and enough water to cover to a boil in saucepan.
- Cook until tender; drain. Arrange in prepared dish.
- Top Brussels sprouts with tomatoes and chives. Season with nutmeg, salt and pepper. Spoon yogurt over layers; sprinkle with cheese and almonds.
- Bake at 350 degrees for 15 minutes or until brown.
- Yield: 4 to 6 servings.

Red Cabbage with Apples and Wine

1 to 2 quarts water
Salt to taste
1 medium head red
  cabbage, finely shredded
4 slices bacon, chopped
1 onion, chopped
2 teaspoons vinegar
1 cup red wine
2 green apples, peeled,
  chopped
Salt and pepper to taste

- Bring water and salt to a boil in saucepan. Add cabbage.
- Cook for 10 minutes or until cabbage is tender; drain.
- Fry bacon in large saucepan until crisp. Add onion; mix well. Cook until onion is brown, stirring constantly. Stir in vinegar gradually. Add red wine and cabbage; mix well.
- Simmer, covered, for 30 minutes, stirring occasionally. Stir in apples.
- Simmer, covered, for 30 minutes, stirring occasionally. Season with salt and pepper.
- Yield: 4 to 6 servings.

Creamed Carrots

1 1/2 pounds carrots, sliced
1 tablespoon sugar
1 1/2 cups chicken broth
2 tablespoons butter
1 1/2 cups whipping cream
1/4 cup Marsala cooking
  wine
Salt and pepper to taste
2 tablespoons melted
  butter
2 tablespoons minced
  fresh parsley
2 tablespoons chopped
  fresh chives

- Bring carrots, sugar, chicken broth and 2 tablespoons butter to a boil in saucepan; reduce heat.
- Simmer for 30 minutes or until carrots are tender and liquid has been absorbed, stirring occasionally; drain.
- Bring whipping cream and wine to a boil in saucepan. Stir in carrots.
- Cook for 15 to 20 minutes or until most of cream has been absorbed. Season with salt and pepper. Stir in mixture of 2 tablespoons melted butter, parsley and chives.
- Yield: 6 servings.

Eggplant Caponata

2 cloves of garlic, minced
1/3 cup olive oil
1 unpeeled medium
  eggplant, cut into
  1-inch pieces
6 tomatoes, peeled, cut
  into eighths
3 medium zucchini, cut
  into 1/2-inch slices
2 green bell peppers, cut
  into 1x1-inch pieces
1 red bell pepper, cut into
  1x1-inch pieces
1 teaspoon salt
1/2 teaspoon pepper
Oregano to taste
1/2 cup sliced black olives

- Sauté garlic in olive oil in saucepan for 2 minutes. Stir in eggplant, tomatoes, zucchini, green peppers and red pepper. Season with salt, pepper and oregano.
- Cook until vegetables are light brown, stirring frequently. Stir in olives.
- Cook, covered, for 1 hour or until vegetables are tender, stirring occasionally. Serve hot or cold.
- Yield: 6 to 8 servings.

Italian Vegetable Sauté

1/4 cup butter
2 medium zucchini, cut
  into 1/8-inch slices
1 (8-ounce) can whole
  kernel corn, drained
1 small green bell pepper,
  cut into 1/2x2-inch strips
1/3 cup chopped onion
1 teaspoon sugar
1/2 teaspoon salt
1/2 teaspoon garlic powder
1/2 teaspoon basil
1/2 teaspoon oregano
1/8 teaspoon pepper
2 small tomatoes, coarsely
  chopped

- Melt butter in heavy 10-inch skillet. Stir in zucchini, corn, green pepper, onion, sugar, salt, garlic powder, basil, oregano and pepper; mix well.
- Cook over medium heat for 8 to 10 minutes or until vegetables are tender and liquid has evaporated. Stir in tomatoes gradually.
- Cook for 2 to 3 minutes or just until heated through, stirring frequently. Serve immediately.
- Yield: 4 to 6 servings.

Vegetarian Jambalaya

Juice of 1/2 lemon
2 cups chopped plum
  tomatoes
1 package Lite Links, cut
  diagonally into 1-inch
  slices
2 tablespoons safflower oil
1 onion, chopped
1 stalk celery, sliced
1 green bell pepper,
  chopped
1 red bell pepper, chopped
4 cloves of garlic, minced
2 tablespoons olive oil
1 1/2 cups vegetable broth
1 cup textured vegetable
  protein
1 cup boiling water
1 (8-ounce) package
  Tempeh, cut into 1/2- to
  3/4-inch pieces
1 cup brown rice
1/2 teaspoon thyme
1/2 teaspoon sage
1/2 teaspoon marjoram
Freshly ground pepper to
  taste
Chili powder to taste
Paprika to taste
Hot pepper sesame oil to
  taste
1/2 cup chopped fresh
  parsley

- Combine lemon juice with enough water or dry white wine to measure 1 cup. Combine lemon juice mixture with tomatoes in bowl; mix well. Let stand at room temperature for 1 hour.
- Sauté Lite Links in safflower oil in wok; drain.
- Sauté onion, celery, green pepper, red pepper and garlic in olive oil in large saucepan until vegetables are tender. Add broth; mix well. Bring to a boil.
- Stir in mixture of textured vegetable protein and boiling water. Add Tempeh, rice, thyme, sage, marjoram, pepper, chili powder, paprika, sesame oil and parsley; mix well. Stir in tomatoes with lemon juice and Lite Links. Bring to a boil; reduce heat.
- Simmer for about 1 hour or until rice is tender, stirring occasionally. May add 8 ounces chopped Seitan.
- This recipe is from John Astin, who played Gomez on the Addams Family.
- Yield: 6 servings.

To keep vegetables fresh longer, line the refrigerator food crisper with 2 layers of paper towels to absorb the moisture.

Creamy Dill Peas

3/4 cup water
1 cup 1/4-inch sliced
  carrots
1/3 cup butter
1 tablespoon cornstarch
1 cup half and half
1 (10-ounce) package
  frozen tiny peas,
  thawed, drained
2 tablespoons finely
  sliced green onions
1/2 teaspoon salt
1/2 teaspoon dillweed
1/8 teaspoon pepper

- Bring water to a boil in saucepan; reduce heat. Add carrots.
- Cook, covered, over medium heat for 8 to 10 minutes or until tender; drain.
- Melt butter in saucepan. Stir in cornstarch until blended. Add carrots; mix well. Stir in half and half, peas, green onions, salt, dillweed and pepper.
- Cook over medium heat for 5 to 7 minutes or until thick and bubbly, stirring constantly. Boil for 1 to 2 minutes or until of desired consistency, stirring constantly.
- Yield: 5 servings.

Mushrooms Florentine

2 (10-ounce) packages
  frozen chopped
  spinach, cooked,
  drained
1 teaspoon salt
1/4 cup chopped onion
1/4 cup melted butter
1/2 cup shredded Cheddar
  cheese
1 pound fresh mushrooms
Garlic salt to taste
1/2 cup shredded Cheddar
  cheese

- Combine spinach, salt, onion and melted butter in bowl; mix well. Spoon into 10-inch baking dish. Sprinkle with 1/2 cup cheese.
- Remove stems from mushrooms; slice stems. Sauté mushrooms and stems in nonstick skillet until brown. Arrange over spinach; sprinkle with garlic salt. Top with 1/2 cup cheese.
- Bake at 350 degrees for 20 minutes or until cheese melts.
- Yield: 6 to 8 servings.

Noodle and Spinach Casserole

1 cup sliced mushrooms
2 tablespoons butter
1 (10-ounce) package
  frozen chopped
  spinach, cooked,
  drained
1 (8-ounce) package
  narrow noodles,
  cooked, drained
2 tablespoons melted
  butter
Salt and pepper to taste
1½ to 2 cups chopped
  cooked chicken
1½ to 2 cups sour cream
1 cup bread crumbs
2 tablespoons melted
  butter

- Sauté mushrooms in 2 tablespoons butter in skillet. Stir in spinach.
- Combine noodles, 2 tablespoons melted butter, salt and pepper in bowl; mix well.
- Combine chicken and sour cream in bowl; mix well. Season to taste.
- Arrange half the noodle mixture in a 2-quart baking dish. Layer chicken mixture, spinach mixture and remaining noodle mixture in order listed over noodles. Sprinkle with mixture of bread crumbs and 2 tablespoons melted butter.
- Bake at 350 degrees for 30 minutes or until brown and bubbly.
- May substitute chopped cooked lamb, beef, veal, ham, turkey or pork for chicken. May substitute canned beef gravy for sour cream.
- Yield: 6 servings.

Stuffed Red Peppers

1 loaf Italian bread, torn
  into pieces
6 large red peppers
2 eggs, beaten
½ cup shredded cheese
1 (3-ounce) jar water-pack
  capers, drained
1 (4-ounce) can chopped
  olives, drained
½ cup olive oil

- Combine bread with just enough water to moisten in bowl.
- Slice top off peppers. Remove seeds.
- Combine bread, eggs, cheese, capers and olives in bowl; mix well. Stuff peppers with bread mixture.
- Fry in hot olive oil in skillet for 15 minutes, turning frequently; drain.
- Yield: 6 servings.

Baked Potatoes with Mushroom Sauce

4 medium baking potatoes
3 tablespoons butter
1/3 cup finely sliced green
  onions
6 ounces fresh
  mushrooms, cut into
  1/4-inch slices
1/8 teaspoon garlic powder
2 tablespoons crumbled
  bleu cheese

- Bake potatoes at 350 degrees for 1 to 1 1/4 hours or until tender.
- Melt butter in skillet. Stir in green onions, mushrooms and garlic powder. Cook over medium heat for 2 to 4 minutes or until mushrooms are tender, stirring occasionally. Stir in bleu cheese. Remove from heat.
- Split potatoes into halves lengthwise. Spoon mushroom sauce over potatoes.
- Yield: 4 servings.

Dilled Mashed Potatoes

8 unpeeled medium
  potatoes, cooked, drained
1 teaspoon each salt,
  pepper and garlic salt
1 tablespoon dillweed
1 cup milk
1/4 cup melted butter

- Mash potatoes with salt, pepper, garlic salt and dillweed in bowl. Beat in milk and melted butter until smooth.
- Yield: 6 servings.

To prepare **Easy Make-Ahead Potatoes**, scoop out the pulp of 8
baked potatoes and mix it with 1 cup sour cream,
1/4 cup butter, 2 teaspoons salt and 1/4 teaspoon pepper. Spoon
into shells and let stand until baking time. Bake at
400 degrees for 10 minutes. Top with cheese if desired.

Lighthouse Inn Potatoes

2¹/2 pounds potatoes,
  peeled
¹/2 cup melted butter
2 cups light cream
Salt and pepper to taste
¹/4 cup bread crumbs
1 ounce Parmesan cheese,
  grated
¹/4 cup melted butter

- Bring potatoes and enough water to cover to a boil in saucepan. Boil until tender; drain. Place in bowl. Chill, covered, overnight. Chop potatoes.
- Combine potatoes, ¹/2 cup melted butter and cream in saucepan; mix well.
- Cook until thickened, stirring every 5 to 10 minutes. Season with salt and pepper. Spoon into 2-quart baking dish. Sprinkle with bread crumbs and cheese. Drizzle with ¹/4 cup melted butter. Bake at 375 degrees until brown and bubbly.
- Yield: 6 to 8 servings.

Scalloped Potatoes

¹/2 cup butter
6 ounces cream cheese,
  softened
1 cup milk
¹/2 cup shredded sharp
  Cheddar cheese
3 pounds potatoes,
  peeled, sliced
1 green bell pepper,
  chopped
1 bunch scallions, sliced
1 (2-ounce) jar chopped
  pimento
Butter to taste
¹/2 cup grated Parmesan
  cheese

- Combine ¹/2 cup butter, cream cheese, milk and Cheddar cheese in saucepan; mix well. Cook until smooth, stirring constantly.
- Layer potatoes, green pepper, scallions and undrained pimento in baking dish, spreading a small amount of cheese sauce between each layer. Pour remaining cheese sauce over top. Dot with butter; sprinkle with Parmesan cheese.
- Bake at 350 degrees for 1 hour.
- Yield: 10 to 12 servings.

Potato Surprise

Boiling water
Salt to taste
4 or 5 medium potatoes,
  peeled, chopped
2 red onions, chopped
2 tablespoons butter
2 tablespoons flour
1/2 teaspoon salt
1/2 teaspoon pepper
1 cup half and half
1 tablespoon Dijon
  mustard
1/2 cup mayonnaise
4 slices crisp-fried bacon,
  crumbled
1 teaspoon thyme

- Pour boiling salted water over potatoes in saucepan. Bring to a boil; reduce heat. Simmer, covered, for 15 minutes or until tender; drain. Arrange in buttered 1 1/2-quart baking dish.

- Sauté onions in butter in saucepan over medium heat until tender. Sprinkle with flour; season with 1/2 teaspoon salt and pepper. Add half and half gradually; mix well. Cook until thickened, stirring constantly. Remove from heat. Cool.

- Stir in Dijon mustard and mayonnaise until blended. Spoon over potatoes. Bake at 350 degrees for 30 minutes or until bubbly. Sprinkle with bacon and thyme.

- Yield: 4 servings.

Swiss Potato Gratin

2 pounds red potatoes,
  thinly sliced
Salt to taste
1 cup ricotta cheese
3/4 cup chopped fresh
  parsley
Freshly ground pepper
  to taste
Nutmeg to taste
1 egg
3/4 to 1 cup cream
1 cup shredded Gruyère
  cheese

- Drop potatoes into saucepan filled with heavily salted cold water. Bring to a boil. Boil for 1 minute. Drain; rinse with cold water. Drain and pat dry.

- Combine ricotta cheese and parsley in bowl; mix well. Season with salt, ground pepper and nutmeg. Beat egg slightly in bowl. Combine egg with enough cream to measure 1 cup. Season with salt, pepper and nutmeg.

- Arrange a layer of sliced potatoes, slightly overlapping, in buttered baking dish. Layer with ricotta cheese mixture, Gruyère cheese and remaining potatoes 1/3 at a time, ending with potatoes. Pour egg mixture over layers. Bake at 350 degrees for 35 to 45 minutes or until brown and bubbly.

- Yield: 4 servings.

Potato and Tomato Casserole

4 cups thinly sliced
  peeled potatoes
1/2 teaspoon salt
1/4 teaspoon pepper
2 tomatoes, chopped
1/3 cup olive oil
1 clove of garlic, minced
3 tablespoons minced
  fresh parsley
3 tablespoons lemon juice

- Layer sliced potatoes, salt and pepper alternately in greased baking dish until all ingredients are used.
- Combine tomatoes, olive oil, garlic, parsley and lemon juice in bowl; mix well. Pour over potatoes.
- Bake at 350 degrees for 45 minutes or until potatoes are tender and light brown.
- Yield: 6 to 8 servings.

Cheesy Caraway Tomatoes

2 tablespoons melted
  butter
1/3 cup coarsely crushed
  butter crackers
1/4 cup shredded Cheddar
  cheese
1/4 cup shredded
  Monterey Jack cheese
1 tablespoon chopped
  fresh parsley
2 tablespoons butter
1/2 teaspoon caraway seeds
1/4 teaspoon salt
1/8 teaspoon pepper
1 tablespoon chopped
  onion
2 large tomatoes, cut into
  tenths

- Combine 2 tablespoons melted butter, butter crackers, Cheddar cheese, Monterey Jack cheese and parsley in bowl; mix well.
- Melt 2 tablespoons butter in skillet. Stir in caraway seeds, salt, pepper, onion and tomatoes.
- Cook, covered, over medium heat for 2 to 3 minutes or until tomatoes are heated through, stirring occasionally. Sprinkle with cheese mixture.
- Let stand, covered, for 1 minute. Serve immediately.
- Yield: 4 servings.

Scoop a small cavity out of a potato and insert a baby
onion before baking for a taste surprise.

Tomatoes Provençale

8 tomatoes, cut into halves
Salt and pepper to taste
8 cloves of garlic, finely
  chopped
3/4 cup fresh bread crumbs
Finely minced Italian
  parsley to taste
3 tablespoons extra virgin
  olive oil

- Arrange tomatoes cut side up in baking dish. Season with salt and pepper. Sprinkle with garlic.
- Sprinkle mixture of bread crumbs, parsley and olive oil over tomatoes.
- Bake for 1 hour or until tomatoes are tender and brown.
- Yield: 8 servings.

Sweet Potatoes Chantilly

6 medium sweet potatoes
1 to 2 tablespoons butter
Salt and pepper to taste
1/4 to 3/4 cup milk, scalded
1 1/2 cups whipped cream
1/4 cup packed brown
  sugar

- Combine sweet potatoes with enough water to cover in saucepan. Cook until tender; drain. Peel sweet potatoes.
- Mash sweet potatoes in bowl. Add butter; mix well. Season with salt and pepper. Add milk gradually, beating until smooth and fluffy. Spoon into baking dish.
- Combine whipped cream with salt to taste. Spread over potatoes. Sift brown sugar over cream.
- Bake at 375 degrees for 20 to 25 minutes or until bubbly.
- Yield: 6 to 8 servings.

Make a hot **Sour Cream Sauce for Vegetables** by heating 1/2 cup
sour cream, 2 tablespoons mayonnaise,
2 teaspoons lemon juice and seasonings to taste.

Sweet Potato Soufflé

1¹/₂ pounds sweet
  potatoes, peeled, cut
  into 1-inch pieces
Salt to taste
¹/₄ cup sour cream
2 tablespoons butter,
  softened
5 egg yolks, beaten
¹/₄ cup shredded Gruyère
  cheese
5 egg whites
¹/₄ cup shredded Gruyère
  cheese

• Combine sweet potatoes, salt and
  enough water to cover in saucepan.
  Cook for 25 minutes or until tender;
  drain. Process sweet potatoes in food
  processor until puréed.
• Combine puréed sweet potatoes, sour
  cream and butter in bowl, stirring until
  butter melts. Fold in egg yolks and ¹/₄
  cup cheese.
• Beat egg whites in mixer bowl until soft
  peaks form. Fold into sweet potato
  mixture. Spoon into buttered baking
  dish; sprinkle with ¹/₄ cup cheese.
• Bake at 375 degrees for 25 minutes or
  until light brown. Serve immediately.
• Yield: 6 to 8 servings.

Zucchini Casserole

1 medium zucchini, thinly
  sliced
1 small onion, thinly
  sliced
2 tablespoons oil
Salt and pepper to taste
3 eggs, beaten
¹/₂ cup grated Parmesan
  cheese
8 ounces ricotta cheese
1 tablespoon melted butter
¹/₂ cup bread crumbs

• Sauté zucchini and onion in oil in skillet
  until tender. Season with salt and pepper.
• Stir in mixture of eggs, Parmesan cheese
  and ricotta cheese. Spoon into greased
  1-quart baking dish. Sprinkle with
  mixture of melted butter and bread
  crumbs.
• Bake at 375 degrees for 30 minutes.
• Yield: 4 to 6 servings.

Vegetable and Polenta Squares

1 small onion, chopped
1 medium red bell pepper, chopped
1 tablespoon olive or vegetable oil
1 clove of garlic, minced
2 medium zucchini, thinly sliced
2 teaspoons basil or dillweed
8 ounces mozzarella cheese, shredded
3³/4 cups water
Salt to taste
1 cup cornmeal
1 (17-ounce) can no-salt-added whole kernel corn, drained
1 (16-ounce) can Italian-style crushed tomatoes, heated

- Sauté onion and red pepper in olive oil in skillet for 5 minutes. Stir in garlic and zucchini. Cook until zucchini is tender, stirring frequently. Add basil; mix well. Stir in cheese.
- Bring water and salt to a boil in 4-quart saucepan over high heat; reduce to medium. Sprinkle in cornmeal.
- Cook over low heat until polenta is thick and creamy, stirring constantly. Remove from heat. Stir in corn.
- Spoon ¹/2 of the polenta into greased 8x8-inch baking dish. Using slotted spoon spread zucchini mixture evenly over polenta. Top with remaining polenta. Let stand for 10 minutes.
- Bake at 400 degrees for 15 minutes or just until heated through. Cut into squares. Top with tomatoes.
- Yield: 4 to 6 servings.

Chestnut Stuffing

6 cups torn day-old bread
2 onions, chopped
4 stalks celery, chopped
1 tablespoon sage, crushed
2 teaspoons thyme, crushed
1¹/2 teaspoons rosemary, crushed
1 teaspoon savory, crushed
¹/2 cup butter
1¹/4 pounds chestnuts, shelled, peeled
¹/2 cup finely chopped fresh parsley
Salt and pepper to taste

- Arrange bread in single layer in shallow baking pan. Bake at 325 degrees for 10 to 15 minutes or until brown, stirring occasionally. Transfer to large bowl.
- Sauté onions, celery, sage, thyme, rosemary and savory in butter in skillet until vegetables are tender. Stir in chestnuts.
- Cook until heated through, stirring constantly. Stir in parsley, salt and pepper. Cool. Stir into toasted bread.
- Spoon into turkey just before roasting or bake in baking pan in oven.
- Yield: 20 servings.

Corn Stuffing

2 tablespoons pork
  drippings
3 cups cubed bread
  crumbs
2 eggs, beaten
3/4 cup chopped green bell
  pepper
3/4 cup chopped onion
1/2 cup chopped celery
Salt and pepper to taste
Poultry seasoning to taste
1 (17-ounce) can creamed
  corn
2 to 3 tablespoons pork
  drippings

- Pour 2 tablespoons pork drippings into 2-quart baking dish, swirling dish to spread.
- Combine bread crumbs, eggs, green pepper, onion, celery, salt, pepper and poultry seasoning in bowl; mix well. Stir in creamed corn. Spoon into prepared dish. Drizzle with 2 to 3 tablespoons pork drippings.
- Bake at 350 degrees for 30 to 35 minutes or until brown and crispy. Serve with sliced roast pork.
- Yield: 6 servings.

Super Sweet Potato Stuffing

1 pound hot sausage
3 tablespoons chopped
  onion
1 cup chopped celery
2 cups bread crumbs
3 tablespoons finely
  chopped fresh parsley
Salt and pepper to taste
4 cups mashed cooked
  sweet potatoes

- Brown sausage in skillet, stirring until crumbly; drain. Sauté onion and celery in nonstick skillet.
- Combine sausage, onion, celery, bread crumbs, parsley, salt, pepper and sweet potatoes in bowl; mix well. Spoon into baking dish.
- Bake, covered, for 40 to 60 minutes or until bubbly. Prepare 1 day in advance to enhance flavor.
- Yield: 6 servings.

Make a delicious **Apple Stuffing** with equal parts
of chopped apples and bread cubes.
Season it with onion, celery, sage and salt.

Calico Rice

4 eggs, beaten
1 (10-ounce) package
  frozen mixed
  vegetables, thawed,
  drained
2¹/2 cups cooked rice
1 cup small curd cottage
  cheese
¹/2 cup grated Parmesan
  cheese
¹/2 cup shredded sharp
  Cheddar cheese
1 small onion, chopped
¹/2 teaspoon salt

- Combine eggs, mixed vegetables, rice, cottage cheese, Parmesan cheese, Cheddar cheese, onion and salt in bowl; mix well. Spoon into greased 8x8-inch baking pan.
- Bake for 40 to 45 minutes or until set.
- Yield: 6 servings.

Rice Chantilly

3 cups cooked rice
1 cup sour cream
1 cup shredded Cheddar
  cheese
Red pepper to taste

- Combine rice, sour cream, ¹/2 cup cheese and red pepper in bowl; mix well. Spoon into 1¹/2-quart baking dish. Sprinkle with ¹/2 cup cheese.
- Bake at 350 degrees for 25 minutes.
- Yield: 6 servings.

꿍

Try one of the newly available and more exotic rices for a
low-calorie side dish. Basmati rice, with its nutty flavor, is good
for pilafs. Jasmine rice is good in warm rice salads.
Arborio is the rice of choice for risotto. Chewy, reddish-brown
wehani is delicious tossed with butter.
Quick-cooking rizcous is good stirred into soups.

Star-Studded Curry Rice

1 cup white wine
1 cup water
1 chicken bouillon cube
1/4 cup minced onion
1/3 cup chopped green bell
  pepper
Seasoned salt and pepper
  to taste
1 cup rice
1/4 cup butter
1/2 cup golden raisins
1/4 cup pine nuts or
  slivered almonds
1/3 cup chopped black
  olives
1/2 teaspoon grated lemon
  rind
1/2 teaspoon curry powder

- Bring wine, water, bouillon cube, onion, green pepper, seasoned salt and pepper to a boil in saucepan; mix well. Stir in rice. Reduce heat.
- Cook, covered, over low heat for 20 minutes or until rice is tender and liquid has been absorbed.
- Melt butter in saucepan. Add raisins; mix well.
- Cook for 3 to 4 minutes or until heated through, stirring occasionally. Stir in pine nuts, olives and lemon rind. Remove from heat. Stir raisin mixture and curry powder into rice mixture.
- Yield: 4 servings.

Risotto Gorgonzola

1 tablespoon melted
  unsalted butter
1/4 teaspoon powdered
  saffron
1/4 cup low-sodium
  chicken stock
1 1/2 tablespoons minced
  onion
1 1/2 tablespoons unsalted
  butter
1 cup rice
6 tablespoons dry white
  wine
3 cups low-sodium
  chicken stock
1/2 cup crumbled
  Gorgonzola cheese
Freshly ground pepper to
  taste

- Pour 1 tablespoon melted butter in shallow baking dish, swirling dish to spread. Combine saffron with 1/4 cup stock in bowl; mix well.
- Sauté onion in 1 1/2 tablespoons butter in skillet until tender, but not brown. Stir in rice. Add wine and saffron mixture; mix well. Stir in 1 1/2 cups stock.
- Cook over medium to high heat, adding remaining stock as needed, until all liquid has been absorbed, stirring frequently. Stir in 1/4 cup Gorgonzola cheese. Spoon into prepared baking dish. Sprinkle with remaining 1/4 cup cheese and pepper.
- Bake at 350 degrees until brown and bubbly. Serve with grilled fish or beef.
- Yield: 4 servings.

Jalapeño Rice

1 cup chopped jalapeño
  peppers
2 cups sour cream
3 cups cooked rice
12 ounces Monterey Jack
  cheese, shredded
Shredded Cheddar cheese

- Combine jalapeño peppers and sour cream in bowl; mix well.
- Layer rice, sour cream mixture and Monterey Jack cheese $1/3$ at a time in 9x13-inch baking dish. Sprinkle with Cheddar cheese
- Bake at 350 degrees until cheese melts.
- Yield: 10 to 12 servings.

Spanish Rice

1 cup rice
1 tablespoon oil
$1/4$ cup chopped scallions
1 clove of garlic, finely
  chopped
$1^1/2$ cups chicken broth
1 green bell pepper,
  chopped
1 (16-ounce) can
  tomatoes, chopped
$1/4$ cup chopped fresh
  cilantro
Salt and pepper to taste
1 teaspoon oregano

- Sauté rice in oil in saucepan until dark brown. Add scallions, garlic, chicken broth, green pepper, undrained tomatoes, cilantro, salt, pepper and oregano; mix well.
- Simmer, covered, for 30 minutes.
- Yield: 4 servings.

Rice bran has a cholesterol-reducing action similar to that of oatbran. The result is attributed to an oil that occurs naturally in the bran and inhibits the body's absorption of cholesterol. It may also decrease the liver's production of cholesterol.

CLASSIC
CONNECTICUT
CUISINE

EGG &
PASTA DISHES

FEDERAL HOUSE • GUILFORD

Breakfast Medley

4 sausage links, chopped
1/2 cup sliced mushrooms
1/4 cup chopped onion
1 tablespoon oil
2 cups frozen home fries, cooked
1 tablespoon butter
4 eggs, beaten
4 slices white American cheese
4 slices toast

- Cook sausage in skillet until brown; drain. Remove to platter. Sauté mushrooms and onion in skillet until tender. Remove to platter with sausage.
- Heat oil in skillet. Add sausage, mushrooms, onion and home fries. Cook until slightly brown, stirring occasionally.
- Melt butter in separate skillet. Stir in eggs. Cook until light and fluffy, stirring constantly.
- Spoon eggs over sausage mixture; top with cheese slices. Remove from heat.
- Let stand, covered, until cheese melts. Serve with toast.
- Yield: 2 servings.

Eggs in Mushrooms

8 jumbo fresh mushrooms
1 tablespoon lemon juice
3 tablespoons butter
2 tablespoons minced shallots
1 clove of garlic, minced
Salt and pepper to taste
1 1/2 teaspoons tarragon
2 tablespoons finely chopped chives
8 small pats butter
8 medium eggs
1/2 cup heavy cream

- Wipe mushroom caps with damp cloth and rub lightly with lemon juice to prevent discoloration. Spread 3 tablespoons butter in shallow baking pan.
- Sprinkle shallots and garlic in prepared pan. Arrange mushroom caps stem side down over shallots. Cook over medium heat for 2 minutes.
- Turn caps over; sprinkle with salt, pepper, tarragon and chives. Place a small pat of butter in each cap. Bake at 400 degrees for 3 minutes, basting once. Break 1 egg into each cap; cover with cream.
- Bake, covered with foil, for 3 to 4 minutes longer or until eggs are done to taste.
- Yield: 8 servings.

Eggs in a Ring

1 egg
1 cup milk
1/4 cup oil
1 cup all-purpose flour
1 cup whole wheat flour
1 cup shredded Cheddar
   cheese
2 tablespoons sugar
1 tablespoon baking
   powder
1/2 teaspoon salt
1 (10-ounce) package
   frozen green peas
1 (10-ounce) can cream of
   chicken soup
3 hard-boiled eggs, sliced
6 to 8 pimento-stuffed
   olives, sliced
2 tablespoons chopped
   onion
1/8 teaspoon poultry
   seasoning

- Beat 1 egg in bowl. Add milk and oil; mix well. Add all-purpose flour, whole wheat flour, cheese, sugar, baking powder and salt; mix just until moistened. Batter will be lumpy.
- Spoon into greased 6-cup ring mold. Bake at 400 degrees for 20 to 25 minutes or until golden brown. Unmold onto serving plate.
- Combine peas and soup in 2-quart saucepan. Cook over medium heat until heated through, stirring occasionally. Fold in hard-boiled eggs, olives, onion and poultry seasoning. Simmer for 3 to 5 minutes.
- Spoon into center of baked ring.
- Yield: 6 to 8 servings.

French Toast

12 eggs
2 cups cream
2 teaspoons sugar
1 teaspoon vanilla extract
1 teaspoon cinnamon
Nutmeg to taste
1 loaf Challah bread
Butter
Fried Banana Syrup (page
   132)

- Combine eggs, cream, sugar, vanilla, cinnamon and nutmeg in bowl; mix well. Slice bread diagonally. Dip into egg mixture.
- Bake in butter on griddle until golden brown on both sides. Serve with Fried Banana Syrup. Garnish with sour cream, strawberries and orange slice.
- This recipe was submitted by Julie H. Barrett, Chef Instructor of Connecticut Culinary Institute.
- Yield: 12 servings.

French Toast Casserole

1 (10-ounce) loaf French
   bread
8 eggs
3 cups milk
4 teaspoons sugar
1/2 cup raisins (optional)
1 tablespoon vanilla
   extract
1/2 teaspoon cinnamon
3/4 teaspoon salt
2 tablespoons butter or
   margarine, chopped

- Cut bread into 1-inch cubes; spread in single layer in greased 9x13-inch baking dish.
- Beat eggs with milk, sugar, raisins, vanilla, cinnamon and salt in bowl. Pour over bread. Chill, covered, overnight.
- Bake, uncovered, at 350 degrees for 45 to 50 minutes or until puffed and light brown. Dot with butter; let stand for 5 minutes before serving. Serve with maple syrup.
- Yield: 8 servings.

Puff Apple Pancake

8 ounces egg substitute
4 eggs
1 1/2 cups milk
1 1/4 cups flour
1/2 teaspoon salt
3 tablespoons margarine
3 large apples, peeled,
   sliced
1/3 cup packed light
   brown sugar
2 teaspoons cinnamon

- Beat egg substitute, eggs, milk, flour and salt in mixer bowl until blended.
- Melt margarine in 9x13-inch baking pan in 350-degree oven. Arrange apple slices over margarine.
- Bake for 5 minutes. Pour egg mixture over apples. Sprinkle with brown sugar and cinnamon.
- Bake for 30 to 35 minutes or until puffed and golden brown.
- Yield: 8 servings.

Fried Banana Syrup can be prepared by sautéing 1 sliced
banana in 3 tablespoons butter until golden brown.
Add 3 tablespoons brown sugar and 1/2 cup (or less) orange
juice and cook until of consistency of syrup.

Ham and Cheese Soufflé

16 slices sandwich bread
16 ounces cooked ham, cubed
4 cups shredded Cheddar cheese
1¹/₂ cups shredded Swiss cheese
6 eggs
3 cups milk
¹/₂ teaspoon onion salt
¹/₂ teaspoon dry mustard
1¹/₂ to 3 cups crushed corn flakes
¹/₂ cup melted butter

- Trim crusts from bread and cut into cubes. Spread in greased 9x13-inch baking dish. Layer ham and cheeses over bread.
- Beat eggs with milk, onion salt and dry mustard in bowl. Pour over layers in prepared dish. Chill overnight.
- Sprinkle with mixture of corn flakes and melted butter. Place in oven with baking sheet or shallow pan of water on lower rack.
- Bake at 375 degrees for 40 minutes. Let stand for 10 minutes before serving.
- Yield: 8 servings.

Overnight Sausage and Egg Casserole

2 pounds bulk sausage
9 slices bread
2 apples, sliced
9 eggs, beaten
1¹/₂ cups shredded sharp Cheddar cheese
3 cups milk
³/₄ teaspoon dry mustard

- Brown sausage in skillet, stirring until crumbly; drain. Spread in lightly greased 9x13-inch baking dish.
- Trim crusts from bread; cut into cubes. Sauté apples in nonstick skillet until tender-crisp.
- Combine bread and apples with eggs, cheese, milk and dry mustard in bowl; mix well. Spoon over sausage. Chill, covered, overnight.
- Bake, covered, at 350 degrees for 30 minutes. Bake, uncovered, for 30 minutes longer.
- Yield: 12 servings.

Overnight Caramel Strata

1 cup packed dark brown
  sugar
1/2 cup unsalted butter
2 tablespoons light corn
  syrup
12 slices white sandwich
  bread
6 eggs
11/2 cups milk
1 teaspoon vanilla extract
1/4 teaspoon salt

- Combine brown sugar, butter and corn syrup in small heavy saucepan. Cook over medium-low heat until brown sugar dissolves and butter melts, stirring to mix well. Spread evenly in 9x13-inch baking dish.
- Trim crusts from bread. Arrange 6 slices in single layer in prepared dish. Top with remaining bread, trimming to fit if needed.
- Whisk eggs, milk, vanilla and salt in bowl until smooth. Pour over bread. Chill, covered, overnight.
- Bake at 350 degrees for 40 minutes or until puffed and golden brown. Let stand for 5 minutes before serving. Cut into servings. Invert onto serving plates.
- Yield: 12 servings.

Broccoli and Bacon Quiche

4 eggs
1 cup half and half
1 cup shredded Swiss
  cheese
2 cups broccoli flowerets
1/8 teaspoon garlic powder
1/4 teaspoon salt
1/8 teaspoon lemon pepper
4 slices bacon, crisp-fried,
  crumbled

- Beat eggs with half and half and cheese in bowl. Stir in broccoli, garlic powder, salt and lemon pepper. Stir in half the bacon. Spoon into 9-inch pie plate.
- Bake at 350 degrees for 30 to 35 minutes or until knife inserted halfway between edge and center comes out clean. Sprinkle with remaining bacon.
- Yield: 6 servings.

Elevate scrambled eggs to a supper omelet with the addition of
herbs, chopped meats or vegetables, dried beef or cheese.

Vegetable and Cheese Pie

3 small yellow squash,
  thinly sliced
1 tablespoon butter
1 tablespoon oil
1 green bell pepper,
  chopped
3 tomatoes, peeled, sliced
3 eggs, separated
2 cups shredded Swiss
  cheese or Jarlsberg
  cheese
4 ounces feta cheese,
  crumbled
Salt and pepper to taste

- Sauté squash in heated butter and oil in skillet until golden brown. Add green pepper. Sauté for 5 minutes. Cook tomatoes in saucepan over medium heat for 2 minutes, stirring frequently.
- Beat egg yolks in mixer bowl until thick and lemon-colored. Beat egg whites in mixer bowl until stiff. Fold into egg yolks.
- Layer half the squash mixture, 1/3 of the Swiss cheese, half the feta cheese, salt, pepper, half the egg mixture, tomatoes, half the remaining Swiss cheese, remaining feta cheese, remaining squash mixture, remaining egg mixture and remaining Swiss cheese in buttered 10-inch pie plate.
- Bake at 400 degrees for 25 to 30 minutes or until set and golden brown.
- Yield: 6 servings.

Herbed Tomato and Salami Quiche

1 unbaked (9-inch) pie
  shell
4 ounces shredded
  Cheddar cheese
2 cups chopped peeled
  tomato, drained
4 ounces thinly sliced hard
  salami, cut into strips
3 eggs
3/4 cup milk
1 tablespoon minced
  parsley
1 teaspoon oregano
2 teaspoons onion powder
1/2 teaspoon garlic powder
1/8 teaspoon ground red
  pepper

- Prick bottom and side of pie shell. Bake at 450 degrees for 8 minutes. Layer cheese, tomato and salami 1/2 at a time in pie shell.
- Beat eggs in mixer bowl. Add milk, parsley, oregano, onion powder, garlic powder and red pepper; mix well. Pour over layers.
- Bake at 450 degrees for 10 minutes; reduce oven temperature to 325 degrees. Bake until set and knife inserted in center comes out clean. Let stand for 5 minutes or longer before serving.
- Yield: 6 servings.

Salmon Quiche

1 cup whole wheat flour
2/3 cup shredded sharp
    Cheddar cheese
1/4 cup chopped almonds
1/4 teaspoon paprika
1/2 teaspoon salt
6 tablespoons oil
1 (16-ounce) can salmon
3 eggs, beaten
1 cup sour cream
1/4 cup mayonnaise
1/2 cup shredded sharp
    Cheddar cheese
1 tablespoon grated onion
1/4 teaspoon dried dillweed
3 drops of hot pepper
    sauce

- Mix flour, 2/3 cup cheese, almonds, paprika and salt in bowl. Stir in oil. Reserve 1/2 cup of the mixture. Press remaining mixture over bottom and side of 9-inch pie plate. Bake at 400 degrees for 10 minutes; remove from oven. Reduce oven temperature to 325 degrees.
- Drain salmon, reserving liquid. Add enough water to reserved liquid to measure 1/2 cup. Flake salmon, discarding skin and bones.
- Combine eggs, sour cream, mayonnaise and reserved liquid in bowl; mix well. Stir in salmon, 1/2 cup cheese, onion, dillweed and hot pepper sauce.
- Spoon salmon mixture into baked pastry; sprinkle with reserved pastry mixture. Bake at 325 degrees for 45 minutes or until set in center.
- Yield: 6 servings.

Swiss Spinach Quiche

1 (8-count) can crescent
    rolls
8 ounces natural Swiss
    cheese sliced, cut into
    strips
1/2 cup grated Parmesan
    cheese
3 tablespoons flour
1 1/4 cups milk
4 eggs, slightly beaten
1/4 teaspoon salt
1/8 teaspoon pepper
1 (10-ounce) package
    frozen chopped
    spinach, thawed,
    drained

- Separate roll dough into large rectangles and use to line bottom and 1/4 inch up sides of greased 9x13-inch baking dish; press edges and perforations to seal.
- Toss cheeses with flour in bowl. Combine milk, eggs, salt and pepper in medium bowl; mix well. Add to cheese mixture; mix well. Stir in spinach.
- Spoon into prepared baking dish. Bake at 350 degrees for 50 minutes. Cut into squares; serve warm.
- May prepared in advance, freeze and reheat if desired.
- Yield: 15 servings.

Zucchini Quiche

4 cups thinly sliced
   zucchini
1 cup chopped onion
1/2 cup margarine
1/2 cup chopped parsley
1/4 teaspoon garlic powder
1/4 teaspoon basil
1/4 teaspoon oregano
1/2 teaspoon salt
1/2 teaspoon pepper
2 eggs
8 ounces mozzarella
   cheese, shredded
1 (8-count) can crescent
   rolls
Mustard to taste

- Sauté zucchini and onion in margarine in 10-inch skillet for 10 minutes or until zucchini is tender. Stir in parsley, garlic powder, basil, oregano, salt and pepper.
- Beat eggs with cheese in mixer bowl. Add to zucchini mixture.
- Separate roll dough into 8 triangles. Arrange in 10-inch pie plate to form pie shell, pressing edge to seal. Spread with thin layer of mustard. Spoon zucchini mixture into prepared plate.
- Bake at 375 degrees for 18 to 20 minutes or until set and golden brown.
- Yield: 6 servings.

Spicy Capellini with Vegetables

1 large carrot, julienned
8 ounces mushrooms,
   julienned
8 ounces snow peas,
   julienned
2 tablespoons olive oil
4 large tomatoes, chopped
1 tablespoon olive oil
1/2 cup chicken stock
1 cup whipping cream
1 tablespoon tomato paste
2 tablespoons finely
   chopped basil
1 teaspoon salt
1/4 teaspoon crushed red
   pepper flakes
16 ounces uncooked
   capellini
1 tablespoon olive oil
1 teaspoon salt
1 cup freshly grated
   Parmesan cheese

- Sauté carrot, mushrooms and snow peas in 2 tablespoons heated olive oil in large skillet over medium-high heat for 3 to 4 minutes or until tender-crisp. Remove to colander to drain.
- Sauté tomatoes in 1 tablespoon heated olive oil in same skillet for 2 to 3 minutes or until tender. Add chicken stock, cream, tomato paste, basil, 1 teaspoon salt and pepper flakes. Bring to a simmer. Cook until slightly reduced and thickened.
- Add drained vegetables. Cook just until heated through.
- Cook pasta in water with 1 tablespoon olive oil and 1 teaspoon salt for 8 to 10 minutes or until *al dente*; drain well.
- Place pasta in large serving bowl; spoon sauce over top. Toss until well mixed. Top with Parmesan cheese.
- Yield: 4 to 6 servings.

Fettucini Almost Alfredo

4 ounces uncooked
  fettucini
1¹/₂ quarts boiling water
¹/₂ cup low-fat cottage
  cheese
1 tablespoon skim milk
1 tablespoon grated
  Parmesan cheese
Coarsely ground pepper
  to taste

- Cook pasta in water in saucepan for 10 to 20 minutes or until tender; drain.
- Combine cottage cheese, skim milk and Parmesan cheese in blender or food processor container; process until smooth.
- Toss fettucini with cheese mixture in serving bowl; season with pepper.
- Yield: 2 servings.

Fettucini with Peas and Bacon

6 shallots, minced
¹/₂ cup butter
8 ounces mushrooms,
  sliced
1¹/₂ cups whipping cream
¹/₂ (10-ounce) package
  frozen tiny peas
16 ounces fettucini,
  cooked *al dente*, drained
1¹/₂ cups grated Parmesan
  cheese
8 ounces bacon,
  crisp-fried, crumbled
Salt and pepper to taste

- Sauté shallots in heated butter in large skillet until tender. Add mushrooms; increase heat to high. Cook until mushrooms are very lightly browned.
- Add cream. Cook for 2 minutes. Stir in peas. Cook for 1 minute. Reduce heat to low.
- Add pasta, cheese and bacon; toss to coat well. Adjust consistency with cream; season with salt and pepper. Serve with additional Parmesan cheese.
- Yield: 6 servings.

Green Noodles with Quick Sauce

1 medium onion, sliced
3 tablespoons olive oil
4 slices bacon, chopped
6 to 8 pepperoncini,
 chopped
2 cups marinara sauce
16 ounces green fettucini
 or other pasta, cooked,
 drained

- Sauté onion in olive oil until tender. Add bacon. Sauté until bacon is cooked but not crisp. Add pepperoncini and marinara sauce. Simmer for 10 to 15 minutes.
- Combine with pasta in serving bowl; toss to mix well. Garnish with Parmesan cheese.
- Yield: 4 to 6 servings.

Eggplant Scallopini Marsala

2½ cups chopped onions
3 tablespoons olive oil
6 cups chopped eggplant
1 medium green bell
 pepper, chopped
12 ounces mushrooms,
 chopped
1 tablespoon dried basil
1 cup cooking Marsala
1 (28-ounce) can whole
 tomatoes with sauce
5 cloves of garlic, minced
Pepper to taste
16 ounces pasta, cooked,
 drained

- Sauté onions in olive oil in large deep saucepan over medium heat for 5 minutes or until tender. Add eggplant, green pepper, mushrooms and basil. Cook for 15 minutes or until eggplant is tender, stirring occasionally.
- Add wine, tomatoes, garlic and pepper. Simmer for 10 to 15 minutes longer.
- Serve over pasta; garnish with Parmesan cheese.
- Yield: 4 to 6 servings.

Roasted Broccoli and Zucchini Lasagna

1 ounce dried shiitake mushrooms
2$\frac{1}{2}$ pounds broccoli, cut into 1-inch pieces
3 tablespoons olive oil or nonstick cooking spray
2 pounds zucchini, sliced crosswise $\frac{1}{4}$ inch thick
2 tablespoons olive oil or nonstick cooking spray
8 ounces shallots, sliced crosswise $\frac{1}{4}$ inch thick
1 tablespoon olive oil or nonstick cooking spray
1$\frac{1}{2}$ teaspoons dried hot pepper flakes
1$\frac{1}{2}$ cups grated Parmesan cheese
4$\frac{1}{2}$ cups Bechamel Sauce (page 141)
16 ounces lasagna noodles, cooked, drained
1 pound mozzarella cheese, sliced $\frac{1}{4}$ inch thick

- Soak mushrooms in warm water to cover in bowl for 20 minutes; drain. Discard stems and press mushrooms between paper towels to remove excess moisture. Cut into $\frac{1}{4}$-inch strips. Place in large bowl.
- Spread broccoli in two 10x15-inch baking pans. Drizzle with 3 tablespoons olive oil or spray with nonstick cooking spray; toss to mix well. Roast at 500 degrees for 5 to 6 minutes or until tender-crisp; add to mushrooms.
- Spread zucchini in baking pans. Drizzle with 2 tablespoons olive oil or spray and toss. Roast for 3 to 4 minutes or until tender-crisp; add to mushrooms and broccoli.
- Spread shallots in 1 baking pan. Drizzle with 1 tablespoon olive oil and toss. Roast in upper third of oven for 6 to 7 minutes; add to roasted vegetables. Sprinkle with red pepper flakes; toss to mix well.
- Reserve $\frac{3}{4}$ cup Parmesan cheese. Spread 1 cup Bechamel Sauce in 10x14-inch baking pan. Layer noodles, vegetable mixture, remaining Bechamel Sauce, mozzarella cheese and Parmesan cheese $\frac{1}{3}$ at a time in prepared pan. Top with reserved Parmesan cheese.
- Bake at 400 degrees on center oven rack for 30 to 40 minutes or until top is golden brown.
- Yield: 8 to 10 servings.

Béchamel Sauce

2 tablespoons minced
  onion
6 tablespoons butter
1/2 cup flour
6 cups milk, scalded
1/4 teaspoon salt
White pepper to taste

- Sauté onion in butter in saucepan over medium heat until tender. Stir in flour. Cook over low heat for 3 minutes, stirring constantly; remove from heat.
- Add milk gradually, whisking constantly. Whisk in salt and pepper. Cook for 10 to 15 minutes or until thickened and smooth, stirring constantly. Strain through fine sieve into bowl; cover surface with buttered waxed paper.
- Yield: 6 1/2 cups.

Vegetarian Lasagna

10 lasagna noodles
Salt to taste
1/2 cup chopped onion
1 tablespoon oil
1 cup grated carrots
2 cups sliced fresh
  mushrooms
1 (15-ounce) can tomato
  sauce
1 (6-ounce) can tomato
  paste
1/2 cup chopped black
  olives
1 1/2 teaspoons dried
  oregano
1 pound Monterey Jack
  cheese, sliced
4 cups cream-style cottage
  cheese or low-fat ricotta
  cheese
2 (10-ounce) packages
  frozen chopped
  spinach, thawed,
  drained
1/4 cup grated Parmesan
  cheese

- Cook noodles in boiling salted water in saucepan for 8 to 10 minutes or until tender; drain.
- Sauté onion in oil in saucepan until tender. Add carrots and mushrooms. Sauté until tender-crisp. Stir in tomato sauce, tomato paste, olives and oregano.
- Reserve 1/3 of the Monterey Jack cheese slices. Layer noodles, cottage cheese, spinach, vegetable sauce and remaining Monterey Jack cheese 1/2 at a time in greased 9x13-inch baking dish. Top with reserved Monterey Jack cheese; sprinkle with Parmesan cheese.
- Bake at 375 degrees for 30 minutes.
- Yield: 8 servings.

Capellini with Lemon and Basil

1 small lemon
1½ tablespoons butter, finely chopped
1½ tablespoons virgin olive oil
8 fresh large basil leaves, shredded
2 teaspoons minced fresh parsley
3 ounces uncooked capellini or thin spaghetti
Salt and freshly ground pepper to taste

- Remove the zest of lemon with vegetable peeler, discarding any white pith. Cut zest into fine julienne strips. Squeeze enough juice from the lemon to measure 2 tablespoons.
- Combine lemon zest, lemon juice, butter, olive oil, basil and parsley in serving bowl; mix well.
- Cook pasta *al dente* in salted boiling water in saucepan; drain.
- Add pasta to sauce in bowl; toss to mix well. Season with salt and pepper. Serve with Parmesan cheese.
- Yield: 2 servings.

Spinach Basil Pesto

1 package fresh spinach
6 cloves of garlic
Pine nuts
Salt to taste
1 cup fresh basil leaves
1 cup olive oil
¼ cup grated Parmesan cheese
¼ cup grated Romano cheese
16 ounces uncooked pasta

- Blanch spinach for 1 minute. Rinse under cold water and press to remove excess moisture.
- Process garlic, pine nuts and salt in food processor until smooth. Add spinach and basil; process until smooth.
- Add olive oil in fine stream, processing constantly until mixture forms smooth paste. Add cheeses; mix well.
- Cook pasta using package directions; drain, reserving a small amount of cooking liquid.
- Combine pesto and pasta in serving bowl, tossing to coat well; add a small amount of reserved liquid if needed for desired consistency. Garnish with chopped tomatoes.
- Yield: 8 servings.

Tomato and Brie Sauce for Pasta

12 ounces Brie cheese
4 large fresh tomatoes
1/2 cup (or more) olive oil
1 clove of garlic, minced
1/2 cup shredded basil
Salt and pepper to taste
16 ounces uncooked pasta

- Remove the rind from the cheese and cube. Chop tomatoes into 1-inch pieces, reserving juices. Combine tomatoes with juices and cheese with olive oil, garlic, basil, salt and pepper in large bowl. Let stand at room temperature for several hours.
- Cook pasta using package directions; drain. Add to sauce mixture; toss to coat well. Garnish with Parmesan cheese.
- Yield: 4 servings.

Macaroni with Vodka Sauce

4 ounces pancetta
1/4 cup butter
1/3 cup vodka
1 to 2 cups tomato sauce
1/2 cup whipping cream
Chopped parsley, salt and
   pepper to taste
16 ounces uncooked
   rigatoni

- Cut pancetta into 4 slices; chop slices. Heat butter in saucepan until foam subsides. Add pancetta. Sauté until light brown. Add vodka. Cook until liquid evaporates.
- Stir in tomato sauce and cream. Simmer for 8 to 10 minutes. Season with parsley, salt and pepper.
- Cook pasta using package directions; drain. Add to sauce. Cook for 20 to 30 seconds, tossing to mix well. Serve with Parmesan cheese.
- Yield: 6 servings.

Add 2 teaspoons of oil to boiling water before adding
rice or pasta to keep grains or strands separate.
A small amount of oil rubbed around the top of the
saucepan will help prevent boiling over.

Pasta with Vegetables and Prosciutto

3 cloves of garlic, minced
1/2 teaspoon dried hot red pepper flakes
3 tablespoons olive oil
3 cups coarsely chopped canned plum tomatoes, drained
1/4 cup chopped fresh basil or 1 tablespoon dried basil
Salt and pepper to taste
2 tablespoons butter
1/2 cup heavy cream
1/2 cup chicken broth
1 cup grated Parmesan cheese
8 stalks asparagus, cut into 1-inch pieces
Salt to taste
Flowerets of 1 bunch broccoli, cut into 1-inch pieces
2 small zucchini, cut into 1-inch pieces
1 cup fresh or frozen tiny peas
1 cup snow peas, trimmed, cut diagonally into 1-inch pieces
16 ounces uncooked pasta
4 ounces prosciutto, cut into thin strips

- Sauté garlic and pepper flakes in olive oil in saucepan over medium-low heat until garlic is tender, stirring occasionally. Add tomatoes. Cook for 5 minutes or until mixture is thickened and reduced to thick purée, stirring occasionally. Stir in basil, salt and pepper.
- Combine butter, cream and chicken broth in saucepan. Bring to a boil; reduce heat. Simmer until reduced to 1/2 cup, stirring occasionally. Whisk in the cheese.
- Whisk the cream mixture into the tomato mixture until smooth; keep sauce warm.
- Cook asparagus in salted boiling water in saucepan for 2 minutes. Add broccoli and zucchini. Cook for 2 minutes. Add peas. Cook for 1 minute. Add snow peas. Cook for 30 seconds or just until all vegetables are tender; drain, reserving cooking liquid.
- Add vegetables to sauce; toss to coat well. Keep warm.
- Cook pasta *al dente* in reserved cooking liquid in saucepan; drain. Add to warm sauce with prosciutto, salt and pepper; mix gently. Spoon onto serving plates; garnish with additional fresh basil leaves.
- Yield: 6 servings.

BREADS

YALE CAMPUS • NEW HAVEN

Cheesy Skillet Biscuits

6 ounces Cheddar cheese
2 cups flour
1 tablespoon baking
  powder
1 teaspoon salt
2 tablespoons chives
3/4 cup milk
1/4 cup melted butter

- Cut cheese into eight 1x2x1/2-inch slices.
- Combine flour, baking powder and salt in bowl; mix well. Add chives; mix well. Stir in milk and butter just until moistened.
- Knead dough 10 times on lightly floured surface. Roll into 9x12-inch rectangle. Arrange cheese slices on half the rectangle; fold to enclose cheese. Cut into eight 2x3-inch rectangles, pressing edges to seal. Place in hot greased 12-inch skillet.
- Cook, covered, over low heat for 10 minutes; turn biscuits over.
- Cook, covered, for 5 minutes or until brown.
- Yield: 8 servings.

Pumpkin Pecan Biscuits

2 cups flour
1/4 cup sugar
4 teaspoons baking
  powder
1/2 teaspoon salt
1/2 teaspoon cinnamon
1/2 teaspoon nutmeg
1/2 teaspoon allspice
1/2 cup butter, chopped
1/3 cup chopped pecans
1 (8-ounce) can solid-pack
  pumpkin
1/3 cup half and half

- Combine flour, sugar, baking powder, salt, cinnamon, nutmeg and allspice in bowl; mix well. Cut in butter until crumbly. Stir in pecans. Add mixture of pumpkin and half and half; mix well.
- Knead dough several times on lightly floured surface. May add additional flour if needed for desired texture.
- Pat dough 1/2 inch thick on lightly floured surface; cut with 2-inch biscuit cutter. Place biscuits 1 inch apart on lightly greased baking sheet.
- Bake at 400 degrees for 12 to 15 minutes or until brown. Serve with butter and honey.
- Yield: 12 to 16 servings.

Sky High Biscuits

2 cups all-purpose flour
1 cup whole wheat flour
4 1/2 teaspoons baking
   powder
2 tablespoons sugar
1/2 teaspoon salt
3/4 teaspoon cream of
   tartar
3/4 cup butter
1 egg, beaten
1 cup milk

- Combine all-purpose flour, whole wheat flour, baking powder, sugar, salt and cream of tartar in bowl. Cut in butter until crumbly. Add egg and milk, stirring just until moistened.
- Knead dough lightly on floured surface. Pat 1 inch thick; cut with 1- to 2-inch biscuit cutter. Place in greased 10-inch cast-iron skillet or 9x9-inch baking pan.
- Bake at 450 degrees for 12 to 15 minutes or until brown.
- Bake on baking sheet for crusty biscuits.
- Yield: 20 servings.

Blueberry Nut Coffee Cake

1/2 cup shortening
1 cup sugar
2 eggs
2 1/2 cups flour
1 tablespoon baking
   powder
1/2 teaspoon salt
1 cup milk
1 teaspoon vanilla extract
3 cups fresh blueberries
1 cup packed brown sugar
1 cup chopped walnuts
1/2 cup melted butter

- Line 9x13-inch baking pan with foil, allowing enough overhang for easy removal of coffee cake.
- Cream shortening in mixer bowl until light and fluffy. Beat in sugar. Add eggs 1 at a time, beating well after each addition.
- Add mixture of flour, baking powder and salt alternately with milk, beginning and ending with dry ingredients. Fold in vanilla and blueberries. Spoon into prepared pan.
- Sprinkle with mixture of brown sugar, walnuts and butter.
- Bake at 350 degrees for 1 hour.
- Yield: 15 servings.

Danish Coffee Cakes

1/2 cup butter
1 cup flour
2 tablespoons water
1/2 cup butter
1 cup water
1 teaspoon almond extract
1 cup flour
3 eggs
1 1/2 cups confectioners' sugar
1 1/2 teaspoons vanilla extract
2 tablespoons butter, softened
1 to 2 tablespoons warm water

- Cut 1/2 cup butter into 1 cup flour in bowl until crumbly. Sprinkle with 2 tablespoons water. Mix with fork until blended. Shape into ball; divide into 2 portions.
- Pat each ball into 3x12-inch rectangle on ungreased baking sheet.
- Bring 1/2 cup butter and 1 cup water to a rolling boil; remove from heat. Stir in almond extract and 1 cup flour.
- Cook over low heat for 1 minute or until mixture forms a ball, stirring constantly. Remove from heat. Cool slightly. Add eggs, beating until smooth and glossy.
- Spread half of the egg mixture over each rectangle.
- Bake at 350 degrees for 1 hour or until topping is crisp and brown. Cool.
- Combine confectioners' sugar, vanilla and 2 tablespoons butter in bowl; mix well. Stir in 1 to 2 tablespoons warm water 1 teaspoon at a time until of desired consistency. Spread over coffee cakes. May sprinkle with chopped nuts.
- Yield: 16 to 20 servings.

For **Quick Sweet Rolls**, dip refrigerator biscuits into melted butter and arrange in baking pan. Make indentation in center of each, fill with jam and bake at 450 degrees for 10 minutes.

Moist Pineapple Coffee Cake

2 (8-ounce) cans sliced
   pineapple
1 envelope dry yeast
2 tablespoons brown sugar
1 teaspoon salt
$1/2$ teaspoon almond or
   rum extract
2 eggs
$21/4$ cups flour
$1/3$ cup butter, softened
Brown sugar to taste
Shredded coconut to taste
8 maraschino cherries

- Drain pineapple, reserving $1/3$ cup syrup.
- Heat reserved syrup to lukewarm in saucepan. Pour into mixer bowl. Add yeast, stirring until dissolved. Stir in 2 tablespoons brown sugar, salt and almond extract. Beat in eggs and half the flour until smooth. Add butter and remaining flour, mixing just until moistened. Beat at low speed for 3 minutes.
- Let rise, covered, in warm place for $11/2$ hours or until doubled in bulk.
- Sprinkle brown sugar and coconut to taste in baking pan. Arrange pineapple, overlapping slightly, over brown sugar and coconut. Place maraschino cherry in center of each pineapple slice.
- Stir dough down. Spoon over pineapple. Let rise for 45 to 60 minutes or until doubled in bulk.
- Bake at 375 degrees for 25 to 30 minutes or until coffee cake tests done.
- Cool in pan for 5 minutes. Invert onto serving plate. Let pan rest over cake for 5 minutes, allowing syrup to drain.
- Cut into squares. Serve warm.
- Yield: 8 servings.

For a brunch treat, butter toasted English muffins, drizzle with honey and sprinkle with almonds. Broil until heated through.

Swedish Coffee Bread

2 envelopes dry yeast
1 teaspoon sugar
$^1/_2$ cup water
1 cup melted butter
2 cups warm milk
12 cardamom seeds,
  ground
$1^1/_4$ cups sugar
$7^1/_2$ cups flour
Cinnamon and sugar to
  taste

- Dissolve yeast and 1 teaspoon sugar in $^1/_2$ cup water; mix well.
- Combine melted butter, warm milk, ground cardamom and $1^1/_4$ cups sugar in bowl; mix well. Add yeast mixture; mix well. Stir in flour.
- Let rise, covered, in warm place until doubled in bulk. Punch dough down. Knead, adding flour as needed for desired texture. Divide into 4 portions. Braid each portion. Place on baking sheet. Sprinkle with cinnamon and sugar. Let rise until doubled in bulk.
- Bake at 350 degrees for 20 to 30 minutes or until bread is brown and sounds hollow when tapped. Remove to wire rack to cool completely.
- Yield: 24 to 32 servings.

Jalapeño Corn Bread

$1^1/_2$ cups self-rising
  cornmeal
1 cup sour cream
$^1/_2$ cup melted shortening
3 eggs, beaten
$2^1/_2$ tablespoons hot
  jalapeño pepper jelly
$^1/_2$ teaspoon salt
1 (8-ounce) can whole
  kernel corn, drained
Cayenne pepper to taste

- Combine cornmeal, sour cream, shortening, eggs, jelly, salt, corn and cayenne pepper in bowl; mix well. Spoon into greased 10-inch cast-iron skillet or baking pan.
- Bake at 400 degrees for 15 to 20 minutes or until brown.
- Yield: 8 servings.

Potato Doughnuts

1 cup sugar
2 eggs, beaten
2 tablespoons oil
1 cup mashed cooked
  potatoes
1 tablespoon lemon extract
4$\frac{1}{2}$ cups flour
1 teaspoon baking soda
4 teaspoons baking
  powder
1 teaspoon salt
1 teaspoon nutmeg
$\frac{1}{4}$ teaspoon ginger
1 cup buttermilk
Oil for frying

- Combine sugar, eggs, oil, mashed potatoes and lemon extract in bowl; mix well. Add sifted mixture of flour, baking soda, baking powder, salt, nutmeg and ginger. Stir in buttermilk.
- Chill, covered, for 2 hours.
- Roll dough on lightly floured surface; cut with doughnut cutter.
- Fry in hot oil until brown on both sides, turning twice. Drain on heavy paper bag. Remove to wire rack to cool.
- Yield: 24 servings.

Blueberry Orange Bread

2$\frac{1}{4}$ cups flour
$\frac{3}{4}$ cup packed brown
  sugar
1 tablespoon baking
  powder
1 teaspoon salt
$\frac{1}{4}$ cup butter, softened
1 egg
2 tablespoons grated
  orange rind
$\frac{1}{2}$ cup milk
$\frac{1}{4}$ cup orange juice
1 cup fresh or frozen
  blueberries

- Grease bottom of 5x9-inch loaf pan.
- Combine flour, brown sugar, baking powder, salt, butter, egg, orange rind, milk and orange juice in mixer bowl.
- Beat at low speed just until moistened. Beat at medium speed for 2 minutes, scraping bowl occasionally. Fold in blueberries. Spoon into prepared pan.
- Bake at 350 degrees for 60 to 70 minutes or until loaf tests done.
- Cool in pan for 10 minutes. Invert onto wire rack to cool completely; slice.
- Yield: 12 servings.

Cheyenne Cheese Bread

6 slices bacon
3³/₄ cups flour
5 teaspoons baking
  powder
1 teaspoon salt
2 cups shredded Swiss
  cheese
¹/₄ cup chopped onion
1¹/₂ cups milk
2 eggs, slightly beaten

- Fry bacon in skillet until crisp. Drain, reserving 2 tablespoons drippings. Crumble bacon.
- Combine flour, baking powder and salt in bowl; mix well. Stir in bacon, cheese and onion. Add mixture of reserved bacon drippings, milk and eggs, stirring just until moistened. Spoon into greased 5x9-inch loaf pan.
- Bake at 375 degrees for 1 hour. Invert onto wire rack immediately.
- Yield: 12 servings.

Cranberry Bread

2 cups flour
¹/₂ teaspoon baking soda
1¹/₂ teaspoons baking
  powder
1 teaspoon salt
1 cup sugar
³/₄ cup orange juice
1 egg, beaten
¹/₄ cup shortening
1 cup chopped walnuts
1 cup chopped fresh
  cranberries

- Sift flour, baking soda, baking powder, salt and sugar in bowl; mix well. Stir in orange juice and egg. Cut in shortening until crumbly. Fold in walnuts and cranberries. Spoon into greased loaf pan, spreading so sides are slightly higher than center.
- Bake at 350 degrees for 1 hour. Remove to wire rack to cool.
- Yield: 12 servings.

Make decorative butter pats to serve with bread by pressing
softened butter into molds or through a decorating tube fitted
with desired tip. Store in freezer until needed.

Cranberry Sweet Potato Bread

3/4 cup packed brown
   sugar
3/4 cup melted butter
3/4 cup mashed cooked
   sweet potatoes
3 eggs, slightly beaten
1/3 cup orange juice
2 1/2 cups sifted flour
1/2 teaspoon salt
1 1/2 teaspoons baking
   powder
1/2 teaspoon baking soda
1/4 teaspoon cinnamon
1/4 teaspoon nutmeg
1/8 teaspoon mace
1 cup chopped fresh
   cranberries

- Combine brown sugar, butter, sweet potatoes, eggs and orange juice in bowl; mix well. Stir in flour, salt, baking powder, baking soda, cinnamon, nutmeg and mace. Fold in cranberries. Spoon into greased loaf pan.
- Bake at 350 degrees for 50 to 60 minutes or until loaf tests done.
- Cool in pan for 10 minutes. Remove to wire rack to cool completely.
- Yield: 12 servings.

Pear Nut Bread

1 (16-ounce) can Bartlett
   pear halves
1/4 cup oil
1 egg, beaten
2 teaspoons grated orange
   rind
2 1/2 cups flour
1/2 cup sugar
1 tablespoon baking
   powder
1 teaspoon salt
1/8 teaspoon nutmeg
1/2 cup chopped walnuts
1 cup confectioners' sugar
1 to 2 tablespoons orange
   juice

- Drain pears, reserving syrup. Reserve 1 pear half; cut into 6 slices. Process remaining pears in blender or food processor until puréed. Combine puréed pears with enough reserved syrup to measure 1 cup. Stir in oil, egg and orange rind.
- Mix next 5 ingredients in bowl. Stir in pear mixture. Fold in walnuts. Spoon into greased loaf pan. Arrange reserved pear slices crosswise over batter.
- Bake at 350 degrees for 50 to 55 minutes or until loaf tests done. Cool in pan for 5 minutes. Invert onto wire rack.
- Drizzle warm bread with mixture of confectioners' sugar and orange juice. Cool completely. Wrap in foil. Let stand overnight before slicing.
- Yield: 12 servings.

Rhubarb Nut Bread

1 1/2 cups packed brown sugar
2/3 cup oil
1 egg
1 teaspoon baking soda
1 teaspoon salt
1 teaspoon vanilla extract
1 cup sour milk or buttermilk
2 3/4 cups flour
1 1/2 cups chopped rhubarb
1/2 cup chopped walnuts
1 1/2 tablespoons butter, softened
1/2 cup sugar

- Beat brown sugar, oil and egg in mixer bowl until creamy. Add baking soda, salt, vanilla and sour milk, beating until smooth. Stir in flour, rhubarb and walnuts. Spoon into 2 greased and floured 5x9-inch loaf pans. Dot with butter; sprinkle with sugar.
- Bake at 325 degrees for 1 hour or until brown.
- Yield: 24 servings.

Carrot Oatmeal Muffins

1 cup flour
2 teaspoons baking powder
1/2 teaspoon baking soda
1/2 teaspoon cinnamon
Salt to taste
1/2 cup packed brown sugar
1 cup milk
1 egg, beaten
1/4 cup melted butter
1 cup shredded carrots
1 cup quick-cooking oats

- Combine flour, baking powder, baking soda, cinnamon and salt in bowl; mix well. Add brown sugar, milk, egg and melted butter; mix well. Stir in carrots and oats. Fill greased muffin cups 2/3 full.
- Bake at 375 degrees for 25 minutes. Serve hot or cold.
- Yield: 12 servings.

Relish Muffins

3/4 cup whole wheat flour
3/4 cup all-purpose flour
1 teaspoon baking soda
1/4 to 1/2 cup sugar
1/2 cup sweet pepper and
    apple relish
2 1/2 cups bran flakes
1 1/2 cups buttermilk
1 egg, beaten
1/4 cup oil

- Combine whole wheat flour, all-purpose flour, baking soda and sugar in bowl; mix well.
- Combine relish, bran flakes and buttermilk in bowl; mix well. Let stand for 1 to 2 minutes. Add egg and oil; mix well. Stir in flour mixture just until moistened. Spoon into muffin cups.
- Bake at 375 degrees for 20 minutes or until muffins test done.
- Yield: 12 servings.

Orange Pancakes

1/2 cup butter, softened
1 cup confectioners' sugar
2 tablespoons grated
    orange rind
1 1/2 cups flour
2 teaspoons baking
    powder
1/2 teaspoon salt
3 tablespoons sugar
2 egg yolks, slightly
    beaten
1 cup milk
1/2 cup orange juice
3 tablespoons melted
    butter
1 tablespoon grated
    orange rind
2 egg whites
Sliced fresh or frozen
    strawberries or peaches

- Beat 1/2 cup butter, confectioners' sugar and 2 tablespoons orange rind in mixer bowl until light and fluffy. Set aside.
- Combine flour, baking powder, salt and sugar in bowl; mix well. Stir in mixture of egg yolks, milk, orange juice, 3 tablespoons melted butter and 1 tablespoon orange rind.
- Beat egg whites in mixer bowl until soft peaks form. Fold into batter.
- Pour desired amount of batter onto hot lightly greased griddle. Bake until brown on both sides, turning once.
- Serve with confectioners' sugar mixture and strawberries or peaches.
- Yield: 4 servings.

Perfect Two-Egg Popovers

2 eggs
1 cup milk
1 cup flour
1/2 teaspoon salt

- Break eggs into bowl. Stir in milk, flour and salt; mixture will be lumpy. Fill greased muffin cups 3/4 full.
- Place in cold oven. Bake at 450 degrees for 30 minutes; do not peek.
- Serve warm with butter or fill with pudding or strawberries.
- Yield: 6 to 8 servings.

Orange Scones

8 ounces cream cheese, softened
1/2 cup sugar
1/3 cup chopped nuts
2 tablespoons grated orange rind
3 cups flour
1 tablespoon baking powder
1 1/2 teaspoons salt
1/2 cup butter
1 cup milk
Honey to taste

- Beat cream cheese and sugar in mixer bowl until light and fluffy. Stir in nuts and orange rind.
- Combine flour, baking powder and salt in bowl. Cut in butter until crumbly. Add milk, stirring just until moistened.
- Divide dough into 2 portions. Roll each portion into 9x12-inch rectangle on lightly floured surface. Spread cream cheese mixture on 1 rectangle; top with remaining rectangle. Cut into twelve 3x3-inch squares. Cut each square into halves diagonally. Place on ungreased baking sheet.
- Bake at 425 degrees for 12 to 15 minutes or until light brown. Remove to wire rack; drizzle with honey.
- Yield: 24 servings.

Cheese Bread

1¹/2 cups flour
1 teaspoon sugar
1 tablespoon salt
2 envelopes dry yeast
1 cup plain yogurt
¹/2 cup water
2 tablespoons butter
6 eggs, at room
   temperature
1 cup flour
1¹/2 cups shredded
   Muenster cheese
4¹/2 to 5 cups flour
¹/2 cup shredded
   Muenster cheese
2 cups julienned cooked
   ham
1 egg, beaten
1 tablespoon milk

- Combine 1¹/2 cups flour, sugar, salt and yeast in mixer bowl; mix well.
- Combine yogurt, water and butter in saucepan. Heat just until very warm, stirring occasionally; butter does not have to melt. Add gradually to flour mixture. Beat at low speed just until blended. Beat at medium speed for 2 minutes, scraping bowl occasionally. Add 6 eggs, 1 cup flour and 1¹/2 cups cheese. Beat at high speed for 2 minutes, scraping bowl occasionally. Stir in 4¹/2 to 5 cups flour and ¹/2 cup cheese or just enough to make a stiff dough.
- Knead dough on lightly floured surface for 8 to 10 minutes or until smooth and elastic. Place in greased bowl, turning to coat surface.
- Let rise, covered, in warm place for 1 hour or until doubled in bulk. Punch dough down. Divide into 2 portions.
- Knead 1 cup ham into each dough portion on lightly floured surface. Shape each portion into a ball. Place on greased baking sheet.
- Let rise, covered, for 1 hour or until doubled in bulk. Brush with mixture of 1 egg and milk.
- Bake at 350 degrees for 30 minutes. Remove to wire rack to cool.
- Yield: 20 to 24 servings.

Panettone

2 envelopes dry yeast
1/2 cup lukewarm water
1 1/2 cups milk
3 eggs, beaten
1/3 cup sugar
1/4 cup butter
1/4 teaspoon cinnamon
1 1/2 teaspoons salt
6 cups flour, sifted
1/2 cup raisins
1/2 cup chopped candied
   fruit
1/3 cup chopped hazelnuts
Confectioners' sugar to
   taste

- Dissolve yeast in lukewarm water in bowl; mix well. Stir in milk, eggs, sugar, butter, cinnamon and salt. Add flour gradually; mix well.
- Let rise, covered, in 120-degree oven for 30 minutes. Stir dough down. Add raisins, candied fruit and hazelnuts; mix well. Spoon into 3 greased 1-pound coffee cans.
- Bake at 375 degrees for 45 minutes. Cool in cans for 5 minutes. Remove to wire rack to cool. Dust with confectioners' sugar.
- Yield: 24 servings.

Rhode Island Pepper Sticks

1 tablespoon sugar
1 envelope dry yeast
1 cup (95 to 115-degree)
   warm water
1 cup flour
1 cup olive oil
2 egg whites, stiffly beaten
1 1/2 teaspoons salt
2 tablespoons coarsely
   ground pepper
4 to 5 cups flour

- Combine sugar, yeast and water in bowl; mix well. Let stand for 5 minutes. Stir in 1 cup flour, olive oil, egg whites, salt and pepper. Beat in 4 cups flour. Add enough remaining flour to make a stiff dough; mix well.
- Knead on lightly floured surface until smooth and elastic. Divide dough into 2 portions. Let rest, covered, for 15 minutes.
- Cut each portion into 16 equal pieces. Roll each piece into a 6 to 8-inch rope. Place on lightly greased baking sheet.
- Let rest, covered, for 20 minutes. Brush with ice water.
- Bake at 450 degrees for 15 to 20 minutes for chewy breadsticks or 20 to 25 minutes for crunchy breadsticks. Remove to wire rack to cool.
- Yield: 32 servings.

Swedish Vörtlimpa

1 envelope dry yeast
1/4 cup lukewarm water
1 1/2 cups stout (beer)
1 tablespoon finely
   ground anise
1 tablespoon finely
   ground fennel
2 tablespoons shortening
1/2 cup dark corn syrup
Grated rind of 1 orange
1/4 cup sugar
1/2 teaspoon salt
4 cups all-purpose flour
2 cups rye flour

- Dissolve yeast in lukewarm water; mix well.
- Combine stout, anise, fennel and shortening in saucepan. Cook until lukewarm, stirring constantly.
- Combine stout mixture with corn syrup, orange rind, sugar and salt in bowl; mix well. Add 2 cups all-purpose flour and 1 cup rye flour; mix well. Add yeast; mix well. Stir in remaining 2 cups all-purpose flour and 1 cup rye flour.
- Knead dough on lightly floured surface until smooth and elastic. Place in greased bowl, turning to coat surface.
- Let rise, covered, for 1 1/2 to 2 hours or until doubled in bulk. Punch dough down.
- Let rise, covered, for 1 1/2 to 2 hours or until doubled in bulk. Shape into two 12-inch loaves. Place on greased baking sheet.
- Let rise for 1 hour or until doubled in bulk. Pierce each loaf 5 or 6 times with fork.
- Bake at 350 degrees for 45 to 50 minutes or until brown. Brush loaves with hot water. Remove to wire rack to cool.
- May bake in 3 greased 9-inch round baking pans.
- Yield: 24 servings.

Reduce yeast bread rising time in half by setting to rise in microwave. Place dough in center of microwave; place 1 cup hot water in corner. Microwave on Low (10% power) until doubled in bulk.

Aunt Mae's Nut Rolls

1¼ cups (105-degree)
  warm milk
¼ cup sugar
2 cakes yeast
1½ cups butter, softened
1 teaspoon salt
4 egg yolks
1 tablespoon vinegar
1 teaspoon vanilla extract
5 to 6 cups unbleached
  flour
Nut or Poppy Seed Filling
  (page 161)
5 tablespoons golden or
  dark raisins
1 to 2 egg whites, beaten

- Combine milk, sugar and yeast in bowl; mix well. Let stand, covered, for 10 minutes.
- Cream butter in mixer bowl until light and fluffy. Add salt, egg yolks and vinegar, beating until blended. Add vanilla; mix well.
- Blend in 5 cups flour.
- Make a well in center of mixture. Pour yeast mixture into well; mix well. Add enough remaining flour to make an easily handled dough.
- Knead gently on lightly floured surface for 5 minutes. Divide dough into 5 equal portions. Chill, covered, for 5 hours or longer. Let stand at room temperature for 30 minutes.
- Knead dough gently on lightly floured surface. Roll each portion into 10x10-inch square. Spread with Nut or Poppy Seed Filling; sprinkle with golden raisins if using Nut Filling or dark raisins if using Poppy Seed Filling.
- Roll as for jelly roll; pinch ends. Place seam side down on ungreased baking sheet.
- Let stand, covered, for 15 minutes. Pierce top and sides with fork at 1-inch intervals. Brush with beaten egg whites.
- Bake at 350 degrees for 20 to 25 minutes or until brown. Remove to wire rack to cool. Cut into slices.
- May substitute canned fillings or poppy seed butter for Nut Filling or Poppy Seed Filling.
- Yield: 50 servings.

Nut Filling

1 pound walnuts, ground
1/2 cup sugar
1/2 cup melted butter
1 teaspoon lemon juice
1 teaspoon vanilla extract

- Combine walnuts and sugar in bowl; mix well. Stir in butter, lemon juice and vanilla; mix well.
- Yield: 50 servings.

Poppy Seed Filling

1 pound poppy seeds,
   ground
1/2 cup sugar
1/2 cup melted butter
2 to 3 tablespoons honey
1 teaspoon lemon juice
1 teaspoon vanilla extract
Sweetened condensed
   milk to taste

- Combine poppy seeds and sugar in bowl; mix well. Add butter, honey, lemon juice and vanilla; mix well. Stir in just enough condensed milk until of desired consistency and taste.
- Yield: 50 servings.

If your kitchen is less than perfect for setting dough to rise,
fill a large bowl two-thirds full with hot water, cover it
with a wire rack and place bowl of dough on the rack. Cover the
dough bowl with a damp cloth to prevent drafts.
To knead bread dough, fold the dough toward you, then push it
away with the heels of your hands in a rocking motion. Rotate it
a quarter turn and repeat until dough is springy and
blistered with tiny bubbles under the surface and smooth on top.

Swedish Saffron Bread

1/2 teaspoon saffron
1 cup lukewarm cream or
   milk
2 envelopes dry yeast
1/3 cup sugar
1/2 teaspoon salt
1 egg, beaten
1/2 cup melted butter
1/2 cup raisins
4 cups flour
Raisins
1 egg, beaten

- Place saffron on small baking sheet. Dry in 250 to 300-degree oven for several minutes. Crush saffron in bowl until powdery. Pour 1 tablespoon lukewarm cream over saffron; mix well. Let stand for several minutes or until saffron dissolves.
- Dissolve yeast in remaining lukewarm cream in bowl; mix well. Stir in sugar, salt, 1 beaten egg, butter, 1/2 cup raisins, saffron mixture and 2 cups flour.
- Beat with wooden spoon until combined. Add enough remaining flour gradually until dough is smooth, but not stiff.
- Knead dough on lightly floured surface for 10 minutes. Place in greased bowl, turning to coat surface.
- Let rise, covered, in a warm place for 1 1/2 hours or until doubled in bulk. Punch dough down.
- Knead dough lightly on floured surface. Pinch off small portions of dough; roll into 7-inch strips. Pinch 2 strips together in center; curl in each end. Place a raisin in each curl. Place on buttered baking sheet.
- Let rise, covered, for 45 minutes or until impression remains when finger is gently pressed into dough. Brush with 1 beaten egg.
- Bake at 400 degrees for 10 to 15 minutes. Remove to wire rack to cool.
- May roll dough thinner and place 3 strips together or roll 1 thick strip in shape of "S".
- Saffron bread is a traditional Christmas sweet bread served with morning coffee on St. Lucia's Day, December 13th.
- Yield: 20 servings.

CLASSIC
CONNECTICUT
CUISINE

DESSERTS

Essex Valley Railroad • Essex

Easter Seals

German Apple Tart

1 cup sugar
3 cups flour
1 cup butter, softened
1 egg
Gingersnap crumbs
2 tablespoons grated
   orange rind
1 tablespoon grated lemon
   rind
1 tablespoon citron
   (optional)
1 tablespoon pineapple
   (optional)
4 or 5 large Granny Smith
   apples
$1/2$ cup heavy cream
1 tablespoon cornstarch
Juice of 1 lemon
2 eggs, slightly beaten
1 cup sour cream
$3/4$ cup sugar
1 teaspoon vanilla extract
$1/3$ cup apricot jam
1 tablespoon water

- Combine 1 cup sugar, flour, butter and 1 egg in bowl; mix well to form dough. Divide into 2 portions. Press 1 portion into 9-inch tart pan. Chill prepared tart pan in refrigerator. Wrap remaining dough in plastic wrap and reserve for up to 2 weeks in refrigerator for another use.

- Sprinkle gingersnap crumbs, orange rind, lemon rind, citron and pineapple in even layer in tart shell.

- Peel apples and cut into halves, discarding cores. Cut small strips crosswise on tops of apples to score them. Arrange cut side down in prepared tart pan. Fill in spaces with pieces of apples.

- Blend cream with cornstarch in bowl. Add lemon juice, 2 eggs, sour cream, $3/4$ cup sugar and vanilla; mix well. Pour over apples.

- Bake at 350 degrees for 1 to $1/2$ hours or until apples are tender but still firm and filling is set. Cool slightly.

- Melt jam with water in saucepan, stirring to mix well. Brush on tart.

- This recipe is from Claire M. Whalley of Gourmet and Contemporary Cooking Instructions.

- Yield: 8 servings.

Whipping cream whipped in advance will not separate if you add $1/4$ teaspoon dissolved unflavored gelatin for each cup of cream.

Finger Baklava

1³/4 cups sugar
1 cup water
Juice of ¹/4 lemon
1 tablespoon honey
1 cinnamon stick
1 cup plus 2 tablespoons
  butter
12 ounces walnuts,
  chopped
¹/2 teaspoon cinnamon
1 package frozen phyllo
  dough, thawed

- Combine sugar, water, lemon juice honey and cinnamon in saucepan. Boil for 5 minutes; discard cinnamon stick. Cool syrup; chill in refrigerator.
- Melt butter in saucepan over low heat. Skim off foam. Pour off clear liquids, discarding solids in bottom of saucepan. Return clarified butter to saucepan and keep warm.
- Combine walnuts with cinnamon in bowl; mix well.
- Spread 2 sheets of phyllo dough on work surface, leaving remaining dough covered with damp towel. Sprinkle with part of the walnut mixture. Place ⁵/8-inch dowel on one side of the pastry and roll moderately tightly around dowel. Place seam side down and press inward from ends with thumb and forefinger to shirr pastry. Remove dowel and cut pastry into four pieces; place on baking sheet.
- Repeat process with remaining pastry and walnut mixture.
- Heat butter until hot enough to make pastry sizzle; ladle butter over rolls. Bake at 345 degrees for 10 minutes. Reduce oven temperature to 325 degrees. Bake for 12 minutes longer or until light golden brown.
- Drizzle chilled syrup over rolls. Let stand until cool. Roll in remaining syrup in pan. Store in refrigerator or freezer.
- May double recipe, but it is best to work with half the ingredients at a time.
- Yield: 40 servings.

Black Cherry Monte Carlo

1 (32-ounce) can pitted
  black cherries
2 tablespoons butter
1½ tablespoons
  cornstarch
2 tablespoons sugar
2 tablespoons cherry
  liqueur
8 slices pound cake

- Drain cherries, reserving juice. Melt butter in saucepan. Stir in reserved cherry juice. Add cornstarch and sugar; mix well.
- Cook over low heat until thickened, stirring constantly; remove from heat. Stir in cherries and liqueur.
- Place cake slices on serving plates. Spoon cherry sauce over top.
- Yield: 8 servings.

Connecticut Blueberry Buckle

¼ cup butter, softened
¾ cup sugar
1 egg
2 cups sifted flour
2 teaspoons baking
  powder
½ teaspoon salt
½ cup milk
2 cups fresh blueberries
¼ cup butter
⅓ cup sugar
⅓ cup flour
½ teaspoon cinnamon

- Cream ¼ cup butter in mixer bowl until light. Add ¾ cup sugar, beating until fluffy. Beat in egg.
- Sift 2 cups flour, baking powder and salt together. Add to batter alternately with milk, mixing well after each addition. Fold in blueberries. Spoon into greased 9x9-inch baking pan.
- Combine ¼ cup butter, ⅓ cup sugar, ⅓ cup flour and cinnamon in small bowl; mix until crumbly. Sprinkle over blueberry mixture.
- Bake at 375 degrees for 35 minutes.
- Yield: 8 servings.

Blueberry Flummery

1/2 cup sugar
2 tablespoons cornstarch
1 1/2 cups water
2 tablespoons lemon juice
1 teaspoon grated lemon rind
2 1/3 cups fresh blueberries
4 orange or lemon rind curls

- Mix sugar and cornstarch in medium saucepan. Stir in water, lemon juice, lemon rind and 2 cups blueberries. Cook over medium heat for 3 minutes or until thickened, stirring constantly.
- Spoon mixture into dessert cups. Chill, covered, in refrigerator.
- Top with remaining 1/3 cup blueberries and orange rind curls. Serve with whipped cream.
- Yield: 4 servings.

Irish Cream Cheesecake

1 cup graham cracker crumbs
1/4 cup packed brown sugar
2 tablespoons baking cocoa
1/4 cup melted butter
32 ounces cream cheese, softened
1 1/2 cups sugar
4 eggs
3/4 cup Irish Cream liqueur
1 1/2 teaspoons vanilla extract
1 cup semisweet miniature chocolate chips

- Mix cracker crumbs, brown sugar, cocoa and butter in bowl. Press over bottom of 10-inch springform pan. Bake at 350 degrees for 5 minutes. Cool on wire rack.
- Beat cream cheese in mixer bowl until light. Add sugar gradually, beating until smooth. Beat in eggs 1 at a time. Blend in liqueur and vanilla.
- Layer half the chocolate chips, cream cheese filling and remaining chocolate chips in prepared crust.
- Bake at 350 degrees for 1 hour. Turn off oven; let cheesecake stand in oven with door ajar for 30 minutes. Chill for 6 hours to overnight before serving.
- Yield: 12 servings.

Flan

6 eggs
2 cans evaporated milk
1 cup sugar
Salt to taste
1 tablespoon vanilla
  extract
1 cup sugar
1 teaspoon water

- Beat eggs in mixer bowl until smooth. Add evaporated milk; mix well. Add 1 cup sugar, salt and vanilla; mix well. Set aside.
- Combine 1 cup sugar and water in skillet over medium-low heat. Cook over low heat until sugar melts and turns light brown, shaking pan occasionally.
- Pour caramelized sugar into 10-inch baking pan, coating evenly. Spoon filling carefully into pan. Place in larger pan of boiling water.
- Bake at 325 to 375 degrees for 1 to 1½ hours or until set. Cool on wire rack. Chill in refrigerator. Invert onto serving plate to serve.
- May decrease vanilla to 1 teaspoon and add 8 ounces cream cheese, 6 slices trimmed and crumbled bread, 1 can pumpkin or amaretto if desired.
- Yield: 8 to 10 servings.

Heaven, I'm In Heaven

1 quart French vanilla or
  coffee ice cream
⅓ bottle of brandy, or to
  taste

- Combine ice cream and brandy in blender container; process until smooth.
- Spoon into individual goblets. May chill for a short time before serving.
- Yield: 4 to 6 servings.

Ice Cream Puffs with Chocolate Sauce

1 cup water
1/2 cup butter
1/2 teaspoon salt
1 cup flour
4 eggs
1/2 cup butter
4 ounces baking chocolate
3 cups sugar
12 to 14 ounces
   evaporated milk
1 teaspoon vanilla extract
Vanilla ice cream

- Bring water, 1/2 cup butter and salt to a boil in saucepan. Add flour. Cook until mixture forms balls, stirring constantly. Remove from heat. Cool.
- Beat in eggs 1 at a time. Spoon into medium mounds on baking sheet.
- Bake at 450 degrees for 15 to 20 minutes or until puffed. Reduce oven temperature to 350 degrees. Bake for 20 to 25 minutes longer or until golden brown and cooked through. Remove to wire rack to cool.
- Melt 1/2 cup butter and chocolate in double boiler over low heat. Add sugar gradually, mixing well. Stir in evaporated milk and vanilla.
- Cook over low heat until thickened to desired consistency.
- Slice cream puffs open, discarding inside filaments. Fill with ice cream. Top with chocolate sauce.
- Yield: 12 servings.

Zesty Lemon Sauce

1 cup butter
2 cups sugar
1/2 cup water
2 eggs, beaten
1/2 cup lemon juice
2 1/2 teaspoons grated
   lemon rind

- Combine butter, sugar, water, eggs, lemon juice and lemon rind in heavy saucepan. Bring to a boil over medium heat, stirring constantly.
- Serve warm over sliced pound cake, gingerbread or blueberry cake.
- Yield: 2 3/4 cups.

Chocolate Mousse

1 cup butter, softened
1 cup sugar
4 ounces sweet chocolate, melted
2 teaspoons vanilla extract
6 eggs

- Cream butter and sugar in mixer bowl until light and fluffy. Blend in chocolate and vanilla.
- Beat in eggs 1 at a time, beating constantly until sugar dissolves and mixture thickens.
- Spoon into parfait glasses. Chill for 3 hours. Garnish with toasted almonds or fresh mint leaf.
- May spread between cookies as cookie sandwich filling and freeze until time to serve. May slightly poach eggs to reduce danger of salmonella.
- This recipe is from Kurt Stiles of the Moose Hopper Coffee Café.
- Yield: 4 servings.

Chatham Village Eatery Mousse

1¼ cups graham cracker crumbs
¼ cup sugar
½ teaspoon cinnamon
½ cup melted unsalted butter
2 tablespoons finely ground toasted almonds
2 cups whipping cream
2½ cups confectioners' sugar
1 cup packed sifted Dutch cocoa
4 egg yolks
1 tablespoon melted unsalted butter
1 tablespoon shaved bittersweet chocolate (optional)

- Combine cracker crumbs, sugar, cinnamon, ½ cup butter and almonds in bowl; mix well. Press over bottom and side of 9-inch pie plate. Bake at 350 degrees for 10 to 15 minutes or until brown. Cool on wire rack.
- Whip cream in mixer bowl until soft peaks form. Add confectioners' sugar, cocoa, egg yolks and 1 tablespoon butter; beat until smooth.
- Spoon into prepared pie plate. Top with shaved chocolate. Chill until serving time.
- May poach egg yolks slightly to reduce danger of salmonella.
- This recipe is from Todd Schrager, owner of the Chatham Village Eatery.
- Yield: 6 servings.

J. P. Daniels Chocolate Mousse

5 egg whites
1/4 cup sugar
2 cups heavy cream
5 egg yolks
1 cup sugar
1/2 cup orange Curaçao
1/3 cup water
6 ounces bittersweet
   chocolate, melted

- Beat egg whites with 1/4 cup sugar in chilled stainless steel mixer bowl until stiff peaks form. Chill in refrigerator.
- Beat heavy cream in mixer bowl until soft peaks form. Chill in refrigerator.
- Beat egg yolks with 1 cup sugar in mixer bowl.
- Heat liqueur with water in saucepan. Stir a small amount of hot mixture into egg yolks; stir egg yolks into hot mixture. Add melted chocolate, mixing constantly.
- Spoon into chilled stainless steel bowl. Fold in egg whites and whipped cream gently; mixture will have a marbled effect. Chill for 1 1/2 hours. Serve in glass bowls.
- Yield: 8 servings.

White Chocolate Mousse

8 ounces solid sweet
   white chocolate
5 egg yolks
2 tablespoons light rum
2 tablespoons water
5 egg whites
1 cup heavy cream,
   whipped

- Melt chocolate in double boiler over hot water. Cool to room temperature.
- Beat egg yolks in mixer bowl until thick and lemon colored. Add rum, water and chocolate; mix well.
- Beat egg whites in mixer bowl until stiff peaks form. Fold into chocolate mixture. Fold in whipped cream.
- Spoon into serving glasses, greased mold or serving bowl. Chill until serving time.
- May poach eggs slightly to reduce danger of salmonella.
- Yield: 8 to 10 servings.

Kahlua Mousse

2 egg yolks
2 tablespoons Kahlua
1/4 cup sugar
3 ounces semisweet
  chocolate
1/4 cup butter
2 tablespoons Kahlua
2 egg whites
1 1/2 teaspoons sugar
1 cup whipping cream,
  whipped

- Beat eggs yolks with 2 tablespoons liqueur in double boiler. Add 1/4 cup sugar, beating constantly until thick.
- Cook over boiling water for 10 minutes, stirring constantly. Place pan in bowl of cold water. Beat until thickened.
- Melt chocolate with butter in heavy saucepan. Stir in 2 tablespoons liqueur. Fold into egg yolk mixture.
- Beat egg whites in mixer bowl until soft peaks form. Add 1 1/2 teaspoons sugar, beating until stiff peaks form. Fold into chocolate mixture. Fold in whipped cream. Spoon into parfait or dessert glasses. Chill for 3 hours.
- Yield: 4 servings.

Crêpes à l'Orange

4 eggs, beaten
1 cup flour
1 cup milk
2 tablespoons melted
  butter
1/2 teaspoon salt
2 tablespoons cornstarch
1 cup orange juice
1/4 cup brandy
1 (11-ounce) can
  mandarin oranges
8 ounces cream cheese
1/4 cup melted butter
1/2 cup marshmallow
  creme
1/4 teaspoon almond
  extract
1 cup confectioners' sugar
1/2 cup chopped almonds

- Combine eggs, flour, milk, 2 tablespoons butter and salt in mixer bowl; beat until smooth. Let stand for 30 minutes.
- Pour 2 tablespoons batter into lightly greased small skillet; tilt to spread. Bake until bottom is light brown. Set aside.
- Blend cornstarch and orange juice in small saucepan. Stir in brandy. Cook over medium heat until thickened, stirring constantly. Add oranges.
- Beat softened cream cheese and 1/4 cup butter in mixer bowl until smooth. Stir in marshmallow creme. Add almond extract and confectioners' sugar; mix well. Fold in almonds. Fill crêpes. Top with orange sauce.
- Yield: 8 servings.

Poached Pears in Rum Sauce

4 firm medium pears
³/4 cup boiling water
¹/4 cup rum
¹/4 teaspoon mace or
   nutmeg
¹/2 cup packed brown
   sugar
¹/4 cup butter
¹/2 cup whipping cream

- Peel pears, leaving stems intact. Remove cores carefully from bottom. Stand pears upright in saucepan just large enough to hold them.
- Add boiling water and rum to saucepan. Sprinkle with mace and sugar; dot with butter. Poach, covered, over low heat for 15 to 20 minutes or just until tender, basting frequently. Remove pears carefully to serving dish; keep warm.
- Stir cream into cooking liquid in saucepan. Cook over medium-high heat until thickened and reduced to desired consistency, stirring frequently. Spoon over pears.
- Yield: 4 servings.

Bread Pudding with Rum Sauce

2 cups light cream
¹/4 cup unsalted butter
³/4 cup sugar
3 eggs, beaten
1 teaspoon vanilla extract
5 cups bread cubes
¹/2 cup raisins
¹/2 cup toasted pecans
1 cup packed brown sugar
¹/4 cup unsalted butter
¹/4 cup dark rum
1 egg yolk

- Scald cream with ¹/4 cup butter in saucepan. Combine with sugar in large bowl, stirring to dissolve completely. Add eggs, vanilla, bread cubes and raisins; mix well. Let stand for several minutes.
- Stir pecans into pudding mixture. Spoon into buttered baking dish. Place in larger pan with 2 inches water. Bake at 350 degrees for 40 minutes or until set.
- Combine brown sugar and ¹/4 cup butter in saucepan. Heat until butter melts and brown sugar dissolves, stirring constantly. Stir in rum and egg yolk. Cook over low heat just until thickened, stirring constantly; do not boil.
- Spoon pudding into serving bowls; spoon rum sauce over top.
- Yield: 8 servings.

Christmas Plum Pudding

1 pound dark raisins
1 pound golden raisins
8 ounces prunes
4 ounces mixed candied
  citron
1 pound currants
1 carrot
1 large apple
1 tablespoon grated lemon
  rind
1/4 cup grated orange rind
12 eggs
1 cup stout (beer)
Juice of 4 oranges
Juice of 3 lemons
1/4 cup molasses
4 cups flour
1 pound bread, crumbled
2 cups sugar
1 teaspoon each nutmeg,
  cinnamon, ginger and
  mace
1 teaspoon salt
1 pound ground suet

- Chop raisins, prunes, candied citron, currants, carrot and apple. Combine with grated lemon and orange rinds in bowl. Add eggs, stout, orange juice, lemon juice and molasses; mix well.

- Combine 4 cups flour, bread crumbs, sugar, spices and salt together. Add to fruit mixture with suet; mix well.

- Spoon into greased bowls. Cover tops with a thick paste of flour and water. Top with greased brown paper, greased side down. Cover with cheesecloth; tie securely.

- Place in large steaming kettle with 2 inches water. Steam over low heat for 6 hours, adding additional water as needed. Remove from kettle and remove cheesecloth, paper and flour paste seals. Store in cool place.

- Resteam until heated through to serve. Serve with soft custard sauce. May pour brandy over pudding to season during storage.

- This recipe was handed down from a grandmother who came from England.

- Yield: 20 servings.

Take advantage of the current popularity of fancy and flavored coffees and serve them instead of dessert. Add a selection of toppings such as whipped cream, shaved chocolate, grated orange rind, cinnamon sticks or grated nutmeg.

Pumpkin Custard

2 eggs
1 (16-ounce) can
  solid-pack pumpkin
1 cup light (20%) cream
3/4 cup packed brown
  sugar
1 teaspoon pumpkin pie
  spice
1/2 teaspoon salt
1/4 cup packed brown
  sugar
1 tablespoon butter,
  softened
1/4 cup chopped pecans
1/4 cup whipped topping
1/8 teaspoon rum extract

- Combine eggs, pumpkin, cream, 3/4 cup brown sugar, pumpkin pie spice and salt in mixer bowl; beat until smooth. Spoon into six 6-ounce custard cups; place in 9x13-inch baking pan. Add hot water to pan to within 1/2 inch of tops of custard cups.
- Bake at 350 degrees for 20 minutes.
- Mix 1/4 cup brown sugar, butter and pecans in bowl until crumbly. Sprinkle over custard.
- Bake for 30 to 40 minutes longer or until knife inserted halfway between edge and center comes out clean. Remove custard immediately from hot water.
- Serve hot or chilled with mixture of whipped topping and rum extract. May store in refrigerator for up to 2 days.
- Yield: 6 servings.

Raspberry Ring

1 (10-ounce) package
  frozen raspberries,
  thawed
2 (3-ounce) packages
  raspberry gelatin
2 cups boiling water
1 pint vanilla ice cream
1 (6-ounce) can frozen
  lemonade concentrate,
  thawed
Blueberries

- Drain raspberries, reserving syrup.
- Dissolve gelatin in boiling water in bowl. Add ice cream 1 spoonful at a time, mixing until melted. Stir in lemonade concentrate and reserved syrup. Fold in raspberries.
- Spoon into ring mold. Chill until firm.
- Unmold onto serving plate. Fill center with blueberries.
- Yield: 8 servings.

Chocolate Raspberry Soufflé

5 egg yolks
3 eggs
14 tablespoons sugar
4 ounces semisweet
  chocolate, melted
2 cups heavy cream,
  whipped
4 ounces seedless
  raspberry jam
1/4 cup water

- Prepare 8 pieces parchment paper sleeves to fit around soufflé cups and extend 2 inches above rims of cups; secure with tape or rubber bands.
- Combine egg yolks, eggs and sugar in mixer bowl; beat until thick and lemon-colored. Spoon 1/3 of the mixture into second bowl.
- Add chocolate to the larger egg yolk mixture; mix well. Fold in 2/3 of the whipped cream. Spoon into paper cone or pastry bag fitted with small round tip. Pipe evenly into prepared custard cups to form shells.
- Blend raspberry jam with water in small bowl. Add to the remaining smaller bowl of egg yolk mixture. Fold in remaining 1/3 of the whipped cream. Spoon into centers of custard cups.
- Freeze until firm. Remove sleeves from custard cups and serve frozen.
- May poach eggs and egg yolks slightly to reduce danger of salmonella.
- Yield: 8 servings.

Unsweetened chocolate or bitter chocolate is chocolate liquid
which has been cooled and molded into blocks for
baking or cooking. Semisweet and sweet chocolate is prepared
by blending chocolate liquid with varying amounts of
sweetening, cocoa butter and flavorings in some cases. Milk
chocolate is the best known kind of eating chocolate.
It is made by combining the chocolate liquid, extra cocoa butter,
milk or cream, sweetening and flavorings.

Swedish Fruit Soup

1 cup prunes
1 cup dried peaches
1 cup dried pears
1 cup dried apricots
1/2 cup raisins
3 quarts water
1 apple, chopped
1 cup fruit juice
2 cups sugar
1 stick cinnamon
1/2 cup red sage
Salt to taste
2 teaspoons cornstarch

- Soak prunes, peaches, pears, apricots and raisins in water in saucepan until rehydrated. Add apple, fruit juice, sugar, cinnamon, sage and salt. Cook for 1 hour.
- Blend cornstarch with enough water to make paste. Stir into soup. Cook until thickened, stirring constantly; discard cinnamon stick. Serve warm or chilled.
- May add or substitute other fruits if desired.
- Yield: 8 servings.

Strawberry Baked Alaska

1 cup strawberry jam or sundae sauce
1 baked (9-inch) pie shell, chilled
1 1/2 quarts strawberry ice cream, softened
3 egg whites
Pinch of cream of tartar
1/4 cup sugar

- Reserve 2 tablespoons strawberry jam. Spread remaining jam over chilled pie shell.
- Beat ice cream in mixer bowl until smooth. Spread in prepared pie shell, mounding in center. Freeze until firm.
- Beat egg whites in mixer bowl until frothy. Add cream of tartar, beating until stiff peaks form. Add sugar 1 tablespoon at a time, beating constantly until glossy. Spread evenly over ice cream, sealing to edge.
- Bake at 450 degrees for 4 to 5 minutes or until light brown. Drizzle with reserved jam; garnish with fresh strawberries.
- May prepare in advance and brown just before serving.
- Yield: 6 servings.

Strawberry Cream in Meringue

6 egg whites, at room
  temperature
1¼ teaspoons salt
1½ teaspoons cream of
  tartar
¾ cup sugar
2 cups whipping cream
Sugar to taste
3 tablespoons Cointreau
1 quart strawberries,
  crushed

- Beat egg whites with salt and cream of tartar in mixer bowl until soft peaks form. Add ¾ cup sugar gradually, beating constantly until stiff peaks form. Shape into 8 shells on baking sheet lined with baking parchment.
- Bake at 250 degrees for 1 hour. Turn off oven. Let meringues stand in oven until cool.
- Whip cream with sugar to taste and Cointreau in mixer bowl until soft peaks form. Spoon strawberries into meringue shells; top with whipped cream.
- Yield: 8 servings.

Godiva Tiramisu

3 ounces Godiva™ Liqueur
½ cup strong black coffee
  or espresso
16 to 20 ladyfingers
1 pound mascarpone
  cheese
2 egg yolks
⅓ cup confectioners'
  sugar
2 ounces Godiva™ Liqueur
2 egg whites, stiffly beaten
3 to 4 ounces dark
  chocolate, grated

- Mix 3 ounces liqueur and coffee in bowl. Dip ladyfingers into mixture and arrange in single layer in shallow dish. Drizzle any remaining coffee over top.
- Beat cheese, egg yolks, confectioners' sugar and 2 ounces liqueur in mixer bowl until smooth. Fold in egg whites.
- Spread cheese mixture over ladyfingers; sprinkle with grated chocolate. Chill overnight.
- May poach egg yolks slightly to reduce danger of salmonella.
- Yield: 8 servings.

CAKES & PIES

GOODSPEED OPERA HOUSE
& CONNECTICUT RIVER • EAST HADDAM

Fresh Carrot Cake

1$\frac{1}{2}$ cups corn oil
1$\frac{3}{4}$ cups sugar
3 eggs
2 cups flour
2 teaspoons baking soda
2$\frac{1}{2}$ teaspoons cinnamon
1 teaspoon salt
1$\frac{1}{2}$ teaspoons vanilla
  extract
2 cups grated peeled
  carrots
1 cup chopped walnuts
$\frac{1}{2}$ cup flaked coconut
1 (8-ounce) can crushed
  pineapple, well drained
Cream Cheese Icing

- Combine corn oil, sugar and eggs in bowl; beat until well blended.
- Sift flour, baking soda, cinnamon and salt together. Add to egg mixture; mix well. Add vanilla, carrots, walnuts, coconut and pineapple; mix well.
- Pour into greased and floured 8x10-inch rectangular cake pan.
- Bake at 350 degrees for 1 hour or until cake tests done.
- Frost with Cream Cheese Icing. Garnish with additional grated carrots and chopped walnuts.
- May substitute 9 or 10-inch bundt pan for rectangular cake pan.
- Yield: 16 servings.

Cream Cheese Icing

16 ounces cream cheese,
  softened
1$\frac{1}{4}$ cup confectioners'
  sugar
1 teaspoon vanilla extract

- Combine cream cheese, confectioners' sugar and vanilla in bowl; beat until well blended.
- May add 1 tablespoon milk at a time to make of desired consistency.

Carrot and Apple Cake

1½ cups sugar
1½ cups oil
3 eggs
2 teaspoons vanilla extract
2 cups flour
2 teaspoons cinnamon
1 teaspoon baking soda
1 teaspoon baking powder
1 teaspoon salt
2 cups shredded carrots
1 cup shredded apples
1 cup golden raisins
1 cup chopped pecans
Cream Cheese Frosting

- Combine sugar, oil, eggs and vanilla in bowl; beat until blended.
- Sift flour, cinnamon, baking soda, baking powder and salt together. Add to egg mixture; mix well. Stir in carrots, apples, raisins and pecans. Spoon into 2 greased and floured 9-inch round cake pans.
- Bake at 350 degrees for 35 to 45 minutes or until cake tests done. Cool in pans for 10 minutes. Remove to wire racks to cool completely.
- Spread Cream Cheese Frosting between layers and over top and side of cake.
- Yield: 16 servings.

Cream Cheese Frosting

6 ounces cream cheese, softened
1 tablespoon milk
2 teaspoons vanilla extract
Dash of salt
1 (1-pound) package confectioners' sugar
½ cup chopped pecans

- Blend cream cheese, milk, vanilla and salt in bowl.
- Beat in confectioners' sugar gradually. Stir in pecans.

Timothy's Black Magic Cake

2 cups sugar
1³/4 cups flour
³/4 cup baking cocoa
¹/2 teaspoon salt
1 teaspoon baking soda
2 teaspoons baking
  powder
1 cup sour milk
1 cup strong coffee
¹/2 cup oil
2 eggs
1 teaspoon vanilla extract

- Sift dry ingredients into large mixer bowl. Add sour milk, coffee, oil, eggs and vanilla.
- Beat for 4 minutes; do not underbeat. Pour into greased and floured bundt pan.
- Bake at 350 degrees for 45 minutes or until cake tests done.
- Cool cake in pan. Invert onto serving plate. Serve with favorite frosting or whipped cream.
- This recipe from Timothy's Restaurant on Zion Street in Hartford is a favorite of all who eat there.
- Yield: 16 servings.

Fig Cake

1¹/2 cups sugar
2 cups flour
1 teaspoon baking soda
1 teaspoon salt
1 teaspoon nutmeg
1 teaspoon cinnamon
1 teaspoon allspice
1 teaspoon cloves
1 cup oil
3 eggs
1 cup buttermilk
2 teaspoons vanilla extract
1 cup fig preserves
¹/2 cup chopped nuts

- Combine dry ingredients in mixer bowl. Add oil; beat until well mixed.
- Add eggs. Beat for 1 minute. Add buttermilk and vanilla; beat until well mixed.
- Stir in preserves and nuts. Pour into greased and floured tube pan.
- Bake at 325 degrees for 45 to 50 minutes or until cake tests done.
- Cool. Invert onto serving plate.
- May substitute strawberry-rhubarb preserves for fig.
- Yield: 16 servings.

Italian Love Cake

1 (2-layer) package fudge
   marble cake mix
2 pounds ricotta cheese
3/4 cup sugar
4 eggs
1 teaspoon vanilla extract
1 (4-ounce) package
   chocolate instant
   pudding mix
1 cup milk
8 ounces whipped topping

- Prepare cake mix batter using package directions. Pour into greased and floured 9x13-inch cake pan.
- Combine ricotta cheese, sugar, eggs and vanilla in mixer bowl; beat until well mixed. Spoon over cake batter.
- Bake at 350 degrees for 1 hour. Let stand until cool.
- Prepare pudding mix with 1 cup milk using package directions. Fold in whipped topping. Spread over cooled cake.
- Yield: 15 servings.

Orange Raisin Cake

1 cup raisins
Rind of 1 orange
1/2 cup butter, softened
1 cup packed brown sugar
3 eggs
11/2 cups flour
1 teaspoon baking soda
1/2 teaspoon salt
2/3 cup buttermilk
1 teaspoon vanilla extract
1/2 cup orange juice
1/2 cup sugar
1/2 cup white wine

- Put raisins and orange rind through food chopper fitted with coarse blade two times; set aside.
- Cream butter and brown sugar in mixer bowl until light and fluffy. Add eggs 1 at a time, beating well after each addition.
- Add mixture of flour, baking soda and salt alternately with buttermilk, mixing well after each addition. Add vanilla.
- Beat for 2 minutes. Stir in raisin mixture. Pour into greased and floured 9-inch square cake pan.
- Bake at 350 degrees for 45 minutes.
- Heat orange juice, sugar and wine in small saucepan until sugar dissolves. Spoon over hot cake gradually.
- Bake for 5 minutes longer.
- Cool cake in pan on wire rack.
- Yield: 9 servings.

Lemon Poppy Seed Cake

4 egg whites
$1/4$ cup sugar
$1/2$ cup butter, softened
$1 1/4$ cups sugar
$1/4$ cup milk
1 teaspoon lemon extract
2 cups flour
2 teaspoons baking
   powder
$1/2$ teaspoon salt
$1/2$ cup poppy seeds
$3/4$ cup milk

- Beat egg whites in mixer bowl until soft peaks form. Add $1/4$ cup sugar gradually, beating until stiff peaks form. Set aside.
- Cream butter and $1 1/4$ cups sugar in mixer bowl until light and fluffy. Add $1/4$ cup milk and lemon extract; beat until well blended. Add mixture of flour, baking powder, salt and poppy seeds alternately with $3/4$ cup milk, beating well after each addition.
- Fold in stiffly beaten egg whites gently. Pour into well greased and lightly floured tube or bundt pan. Bake at 350 degrees for 1 hour and 15 minutes or until cake tests done. Cool in pan for 5 minutes. Invert onto wire rack to cool completely.
- Frost with favorite frosting or sprinkle with confectioners' sugar.
- Yield: 16 servings.

Pineapple Upside-Down Cake

$1/2$ cup (about) packed
   brown sugar
1 (20-ounce) can sliced
   pineapple
1 cup margarine, softened
$1 1/2$ cups sugar
4 eggs
1 tablespoon vanilla extract
$1/2$ cup milk
2 large carrots, grated
6 ounces grated coconut
2 cups flour
1 tablespoon baking
   powder
$1/8$ teaspoon salt

- Butter springform pan; sprinkle bottom with brown sugar. Drain pineapple; arrange slices in prepared pan. Set aside.
- Cream margarine and sugar in mixer bowl. Beat in eggs 1 at a time.
- Add vanilla, milk, carrots and coconut, mixing well after each addition.
- Add mixture of flour, baking powder and salt; mix well. Pour over pineapple slices.
- Bake at 350 degrees for 1 hour or until cake tests done.
- Invert onto serving plate. Remove side and bottom of pan.
- Yield: 12 servings.

Plum Spice Cake Roll

4 egg whites
1/4 teaspoon cream of
  tartar
3/4 cup sugar
4 egg yolks, beaten
1/2 teaspoon vanilla extract
1/2 cup flour
1/2 teaspoon baking
  powder
1/4 teaspoon salt
1/8 teaspoon cinnamon
1/8 teaspoon nutmeg
1/8 teaspoon allspice
Confectioners' sugar
1 cup sieved cottage
  cheese
4 ounces cream cheese,
  softened
1/4 cup confectioners'
  sugar
1 tablespoon lemon juice
1/2 teaspoon grated lemon
  rind
2 cups thinly sliced fresh
  plums

- Beat egg whites with cream of tartar in mixer bowl until soft peaks form. Add sugar gradually, beating until glossy.
- Fold in egg yolks beaten with vanilla and mixture of next 6 ingredients. Spread evenly in waxed paper-lined 10x15-inch cake pan. Bake at 375 degrees for 12 to 15 minutes or until cake tests done.
- Loosen cake from sides of pan. Invert onto towel dusted with confectioners' sugar. Peel off waxed paper; trim off crisp edges. Roll as for jelly roll in towel from narrow end. Cool on wire rack.
- Beat cottage cheese, cream cheese, 1/4 cup confectioners' sugar, lemon juice and lemon rind in bowl until creamy.
- Unroll cake; remove towel. Spread cake with cheese mixture. Reserve several plum slices for garnish. Arrange remaining plum slices over cheese layer. Reroll cake. Place on serving plate.
- Garnish with dusting of confectioners' sugar and reserved plum slices. Chill for several hours before serving.
- Yield: 8 servings.

Blueberry and Rhubarb Pie

2 cups blueberries
2 cups 1/4-inch rhubarb
  pieces
1 1/2 cups sugar
3 tablespoons flour
1/4 teaspoon nutmeg
1/8 teaspoon salt
1/4 teaspoon cinnamon
2 tablespoons lemon juice
1 unbaked (9-inch)
  deep-dish pie shell

- Combine blueberries, rhubarb, sugar, flour, nutmeg, salt, cinnamon and lemon juice in large bowl; mix gently. Spoon into pie shell.
- Bake at 450 degrees for 10 minutes. Reduce temperature to 350 degrees. Bake for 40 to 45 minutes longer.
- Yield: 8 servings.

Triple Chocolate Brownie Pie

2 eggs
1 cup sugar
1/2 cup butter, softened
1/2 cup flour
1/3 cup baking cocoa
1/4 teaspoon salt
1 teaspoon vanilla extract
1/2 cup chocolate chips
1/2 cup chopped nuts

- Beat eggs in bowl. Add sugar and butter; beat until well blended.
- Add mixture of flour, cocoa and salt; mix well. Stir in vanilla, chocolate chips and nuts.
- Spread evenly in greased 8 or 9-inch pie plate.
- Bake at 350 degrees for 35 minutes or until set; pie should not test done in center.
- Cool completely before cutting into wedges.
- Serve with vanilla ice cream and chocolate syrup.
- Yield: 8 servings.

Marbled Chocolate Mint Pie

1/4 cup chocolate syrup
1 (14-ounce) can sweetened condensed milk
1 cup whipping cream, whipped
1 tablespoon Creme de Menthe
1 chocolate crumb pie shell

- Blend chocolate syrup with 1 cup condensed milk in bowl. Fold in half the whipped cream gently.
- Blend remaining condensed milk with Creme de Menthe in small bowl. Fold in remaining whipped cream.
- Swirl mint mixture gently into chocolate mixture. Pour into pie shell.
- Freeze for 6 hours or until firm.
- Garnish with chocolate curls.
- Yield: 8 servings.

Unique Peach Pie

3/4 cup flour
1 teaspoon baking powder
1/2 teaspoon salt
1 (3-ounce) package
  vanilla pudding and pie
  filling mix
3 tablespoons butter,
  softened
1 egg
1/2 cup milk
1 (28-ounce) can sliced
  peaches
8 ounces cream cheese,
  softened
1/2 cup sugar
1/2 teaspoon cinnamon
1 tablespoon sugar

- Combine flour, baking powder, salt, pudding mix, butter, egg and milk in mixer bowl. Beat at medium speed for 2 minutes. Pour into greased pie plate.
- Drain peaches, reserving juice. Arrange peach slices over batter.
- Combine cream cheese, 1/2 cup sugar and 1 tablespoon reserved peach juice in small mixer bowl. Beat at medium speed for 2 minutes.
- Spoon over peaches to within 1 inch of edge of pie plate. Sprinkle with mixture of cinnamon and 1 tablespoon sugar.
- Bake at 350 degrees for 30 to 35 minutes. Let stand until cool.
- Chill until serving time.
- Do not use instant pudding mix.
- Yield: 8 servings.

Streusel Pear Pie

1/2 cup sugar
1 teaspoon cinnamon
2 tablespoons lemon juice
1 1/2 tablespoons
  quick-cooking tapioca
6 cups sliced peeled
  Bartlett pears
1 unbaked (9-inch) pie
  shell
1/2 cup butter
1/2 cup packed brown
  sugar
1 cup flour

- Combine sugar, cinnamon, lemon juice and tapioca in large bowl; mix well. Add pears; mix until pears slices are coated. Let stand for 15 minutes. Pour into pie shell.
- Combine butter, brown sugar and flour in small bowl; mix until crumbly. Sprinkle over pear mixture.
- Bake at 375 degrees for 45 to 50 minutes or until crust is golden brown.
- Serve warm or cold.
- Yield: 8 servings.

Peanut Butter Pie

1 cup graham cracker
  crumbs
1/4 cup sugar
1/4 cup unsalted butter,
  cut up, softened
8 ounces cream cheese,
  softened
1 cup creamy peanut butter
1 cup confectioners' sugar
2 tablespoons unsalted
  butter, softened
1/2 cup whipping cream,
  whipped
2 tablespoons
  confectioners' sugar
1 tablespoon vanilla extract
1/2 cup whipping cream
6 ounces semisweet
  chocolate, chopped

- Combine crumbs, 1/4 cup sugar and 1/4 cup butter in bowl; mix well. Press over bottom and side of buttered 9-inch pie plate. Chill for 1 hour.
- Beat cream cheese and peanut butter in large mixer bowl until blended. Add 1 cup confectioners' sugar and 2 tablespoons butter. Beat until light and fluffy. Set aside.
- Beat whipped cream with 2 tablespoons confectioners' sugar and vanilla. Fold 1/3 at a time into peanut butter mixture. Spoon into pie shell. Chill until firm. Bring 1/2 cup whipping cream to a simmer in heavy saucepan. Add chocolate. Heat until melted, stirring constantly. Cool to lukewarm. Spread over peanut butter layer. Chill until firm.
- Yield: 8 servings.

Pumpkin and Apple Pie

1/4 cup butter
3 medium apples, peeled,
  coarsely chopped
1 teaspoon cinnamon
1/4 teaspoon allspice
1/4 teaspoon nutmeg
1 tablespoon flour
1/4 cup apple juice
2 tablespoons sugar
1 unbaked (9-inch) pie
  shell
1 cup pumpkin
1 egg
1/3 cup sugar
1/2 teaspoon cinnamon
1/4 teaspoon nutmeg
1/4 teaspoon cloves
1/2 cup half and half

- Melt butter in skillet over medium heat. Add apples, 1 teaspoon cinnamon, allspice and nutmeg. Sauté for 5 minutes.
- Stir in flour, apple juice and 2 tablespoons sugar. Pour into pie shell.
- Combine pumpkin, egg, 1/3 cup sugar, remaining spices and half and half in medium bowl; mix well. Pour over apple mixture carefully.
- Bake at 425 degrees for 15 minutes. Reduce temperature to 350 degrees. Bake for 30 minutes longer or until set in center.
- Yield: 8 servings.

CANDY & COOKIES

CORNER OF CHURCH AND CHAPEL 1907 • NEW HAVEN

Cashew Toffee

1 tablespoon butter,
  softened
1 cup chopped cashews
1 cup butter
2 cups sugar
2 tablespoons light corn
  syrup
2 tablespoons water
1/8 teaspoon cream of
  taratar
1 teaspoon vanilla extract
2 cups semisweet
  chocolate chips
1/4 cup chopped cashews

- Line 10x15-inch baking pan with foil. Coat with 1 tablespoon butter. Sprinkle 1 cup cashews evenly in prepared pan.
- Microwave 1 cup butter in 8-cup glass measure on High for 1 1/2 to 2 minutes or until melted. Stir in sugar, corn syrup, water and cream of tartar.
- Microwave on High for 5 1/2 minutes or to 290 degrees on candy thermometer, soft crack stage. Stir in vanilla.
- Pour evenly over cashews. Sprinkle with chocolate chips. Let stand for 1 minute or until softened. Spread chocolate over toffee. Sprinkle with 1/4 cup cashews.
- Cool. Break into pieces. Store in airtight container.
- Yield: 2 1/2 pounds.

Chocolate Amaretto Balls

3 cups semisweet
  chocolate chips
1 (14-ounce) can
  sweetened condensed
  milk
3 tablespoons Amaretto
1/2 teaspoon almond
  extract
2 cups (about) finely
  chopped almonds

- Combine chocolate chips and condensed milk in saucepan over low heat. Heat until chocolate melts, stirring constantly. Remove from heat. Stir in Amaretto and almond extract. Chill for 2 hours.
- Shape into 3/4-inch balls; roll in almonds. Place on tray. Chill until firm.
- Store at room temperature in lightly covered container for 24 hours before serving.
- May vary recipe to make Chocolate Rum Balls by omitting Amaretto, almond extract and almonds and stirring 1/4 cup dark rum into chocolate mixture, proceeding as above and rolling balls in flaked coconut.
- Yield: 6 dozen.

Mint Swirl Fudge

1 tablespoon shortening
3 ounces cream cheese
1 (14-ounce) can
  sweetened condensed
  milk
1/4 teaspoon mint extract
1 or 2 drops of green food
  coloring
3 cups semisweet
  chocolate chips
1 tablespoon butter
1/2 teaspoon vanilla extract

- Line 8-inch square dish with foil; coat with shortening.
- Microwave cream cheese in medium microwave-safe mixer bowl on High for 15 to 30 seconds or until softened.
- Add 2 tablespoons condensed milk, mint extract and food coloring. Beat at low speed until smooth. Set aside.
- Combine remaining condensed milk, chocolate chips and butter in 8-cup microwave-safe measure. Microwave on Medium (50% power) for 2 to 3 1/2 minutes or until mixture is glossy and smooth, stirring twice. Stir in vanilla.
- Pour into prepared pan. Smooth top with spatula.
- Drop cream cheese mixture by spoonfuls over chocolate mixture. Swirl decoratively with spatula. Garnish with sprinkle of green-colored sugar.
- Chill until firm. Cut into squares. Store in cool dry place.
- Yield: 2 1/4 pounds.

Peanut Butter Nougats

1/2 cup crunchy peanut
  butter
2/3 cup sweetened
  condensed milk
1 3/4 cups confectioners'
  sugar
1 cup seedless raisins
1 teaspoon grated orange
  rind

- Blend peanut butter and condensed milk in bowl.
- Add confectioners' sugar; mix well. Stir in raisins and orange rind.
- Shape into small balls; place on plate.
- Chill overnight. Wrap individually in plastic wrap or foil.
- Nougats will keep for as long as 2 weeks.
- Yield: 3 dozen.

Peanut Clusters

1¹/3 cups chocolate chips
1 tablespoon oil
1 cup golden raisins
1 cup peanuts

- Combine chocolate chips and oil in small saucepan over low heat. Heat until chocolate melts, stirring constantly. Remove from heat.
- Add raisins and peanuts; mix well. Drop by spoonfuls onto greased tray.
- Chill until firm.
- Clusters will keep for 3 weeks.
- Yield: 1 dozen.

Bourbon Balls

1 cup chocolate chips
1 tablespoon honey
2 tablespoons bourbon
1 cup chopped nuts
1¹/4 cups crushed vanilla
  wafers or Lorna Doones
1 cup (about) sugar

- Combine chocolate chips and honey in microwave-safe bowl. Microwave on High for 1 to 2 minutes or until melted. Stir until well blended.
- Add bourbon and nuts; mix well. Add cookie crumbs; mix well.
- Shape into walnut-sized balls; roll in sugar to coat. Place on tray.
- Store in airtight container.
- Yield: 2¹/2 dozen.

Rum Balls

1 (12-ounce) package
  vanilla wafers
1 cup finely ground nuts
3 tablespoons baking
  cocoa
¹/2 cup rum
1 cup confectioners' sugar

- Crush vanilla wafers into fine crumbs; place in bowl.
- Add nuts and cocoa; mix well. Add rum; mix well.
- Spread confectioners' sugar on foil. Shape crumb mixture into small balls; roll in confectioners' sugar to coat.
- Refrigerate in airtight container.
- Yield: 2 to 3 dozen.

Anginettes

1 cup shortening
1 cup sugar
4 eggs, beaten
1 cup orange juice
6 cups flour
2 tablespoons baking
    powder
1 teaspoon baking soda
2 cups confectioners' sugar
1/4 cup water
2 teaspoons anise, almond
    or vanilla extract

- Cream shortening and sugar in bowl. Add eggs and orange juice; mix well.
- Mix flour, baking powder and baking soda together. Add to orange juice mixture gradually, mixing well after each addition. May add additional flour if dough is too sticky.
- Shape dough into small balls; place on lightly greased cookie sheet.
- Bake at 350 degrees for 10 minutes or until bottoms of cookies are light brown. Cool on wire rack.
- Combine confectioners' sugar, water and flavoring in bowl; mix until smooth.
- Dip tops of cooled cookies into frosting; place on wire rack to dry.
- May color frosting if desired or sprinkle frosted cookies with colored sprinkles.
- Yield: 6 to 8 dozen.

Apple Cheddar Cookies

1/2 cup butter, softened
1/2 cup sugar
1 egg
1 teaspoon vanilla extract
11/2 cups flour
1/2 teaspoon baking soda
1/2 teaspoon cinnamon
1/2 teaspoon salt
11/2 cups shredded
    Cheddar cheese
11/2 cups chopped peeled
    apples
1/4 cup chopped nuts

- Cream butter and sugar in bowl until light and fluffy. Add egg and vanilla; mix well.
- Mix flour, baking soda, cinnamon and salt together. Add to creamed mixture; mix well.
- Add cheese, apples and nuts; mix well.
- Drop by teaspoonfuls onto ungreased cookie sheet.
- Bake at 375 degrees for 15 minutes. Cool on wire rack.
- Yield: 41/2 dozen.

Beer Brownies

1 cup sifted cake flour
1/2 cup baking cocoa
1/2 cup butter, softened
1 1/4 cups packed brown sugar
2 eggs
1/8 teaspoon salt
1/2 cup beer, non-alcoholic beer or seltzer
1 cup chopped walnuts

- Sift flour and cocoa together; set aside.
- Cream butter in bowl. Add brown sugar gradually, creaming until light and fluffy.
- Add eggs and salt; blend well.
- Add flour mixture and beer alternately, mixing well after each addition. Stir in walnuts.
- Pour into greased 8-inch square brownie pan.
- Bake at 350 degrees for 30 minutes or until brownies test done.
- Yield: 12 to 16 squares.

Chocolate Almond Crunch

1/2 cup packed light brown sugar
1/2 cup margarine
2 tablespoons corn syrup
1 (10-ounce) package slivered almonds
8 to 10 tablespoons flour
1 cup chocolate chips

- Combine brown sugar, margarine and corn syrup in saucepan. Cook over low heat until well blended, stirring constantly. Remove from heat.
- Add almonds and enough flour to make dough of desired consistency; mix well.
- Drop by teaspoonfuls onto ungreased cookie sheet.
- Bake at 350 degrees for 7 to 10 minutes or until light golden color.
- Cool on cookie sheet for 1 to 2 minutes; remove carefully with spatula and place flat side up on wire rack to cool completely.
- Melt chocolate chips in double boiler over hot water.
- Spread chocolate over flat side of cookies; place on tray.
- Place in freezer for 10 minutes or until chocolate is set.
- Yield: 8 dozen.

Chocolate Biscotti

4²/3 cups flour
1 cup baking cocoa
2 cups sugar
1 tablespoon baking
    powder
1 teaspoon baking soda
1/8 teaspoon salt
6 eggs
6 egg whites
1 cup oil
2 teaspoons vanilla extract

- Combine flour, cocoa, sugar, baking powder, baking soda and salt in large bowl; mix well. Add eggs, egg whites, oil and vanilla; mix until mixture forms ball.
- Shape into two 2-inch diameter logs on lightly floured surface. Place on cookie sheet.
- Bake at 350 degrees for 25 to 30 minutes. Cool for 10 minutes. Slice diagonally 1 inch thick. Arrange cut side down on cookie sheet. Bake for 5 minutes. Turn slices over. Bake for 5 minutes longer. Remove to wire rack to cool.
- Yield: 3 dozen.

Cream Wafers

1 cup butter, softened
1/3 cup whipping cream
2 cups flour
1 cup (or more) sugar
1/4 cup butter, softened
3/4 cup sifted
    confectioners' sugar
1 egg yolk
1 teaspoon vanilla extract

- Combine 1 cup butter, cream and flour in bowl; mix well. Chill for 1 hour.
- Roll 1/8 inch thick on lightly floured surface; cut into 1¹/2-inch rounds. Place rounds on waxed paper; sprinkle generously with sugar, turning to coat both sides. Arrange on ungreased cookie sheet. Prick each in 4 places with fork.
- Bake at 375 degrees for 7 to 9 minutes. Remove to wire rack to cool.
- Beat remaining ingredients in bowl until creamy. Tint with food coloring if desired.
- Frost half the cookies; top with the remaining cookies. Use a light hand when assembling cookies as they are delicate.
- May poach eggs slightly to reduce danger of salmonella.
- Yield: 1¹/2 dozen.

Crumpets

1 cup packed brown sugar
1/2 cup butter
1 egg
2 tablespoons sour cream
1 teaspoon vanilla extract
2 cups flour
1/2 teaspoon baking soda
1 cup raisins or chocolate
   chips

- Cream brown sugar and butter in bowl until smooth. Beat in egg.
- Add sour cream and vanilla; blend well. Add mixture of flour and baking soda; mix well. Stir in raisins.
- Drop by tablespoonfuls onto lightly greased cookie sheet.
- Bake at 375 degrees for 12 minutes. Cool on wire rack.
- Yield: 3 to 4 dozen.

Honey and Spice Cookies

2 cups flour
3/4 cup sugar
1/4 cup butter, softened
1/4 cup honey
1 egg
1/2 teaspoon salt
1/2 teaspoon baking soda
1/2 teaspoon nutmeg
1/4 teaspoon cloves
1/2 teaspoon orange extract
1 cup confectioners' sugar
2 tablespoons milk
2 teaspoons grated orange
   rind

- Combine flour, sugar, butter, honey, egg, salt, baking soda, spices and orange extract in mixer bowl. Beat at low speed for 1 to 2 minutes or until well mixed.
- Drop by rounded teaspoonfuls 2 inches apart onto ungreased cookie sheet.
- Bake at 375 degrees for 7 to 10 minutes or until lightly browned on edges.
- Blend confectioners' sugar with milk and orange rind in small bowl.
- Dip or frost warm cookies with glaze.
- Yield: 3 dozen.

Macaroons

1 loaf sliced white bread
1 or 2 (14-ounce) cans
  sweetened condensed
  milk
1 or 2 packages shredded
  or flaked coconut

- Trim crusts from bread slices; cut each slice into 6 strips.
- Dip each strip in condensed milk; roll in coconut to coat.
- Arrange on cookie sheet; do not allow strips to touch.
- Bake at 350 degrees for 5 minutes. Turn strips over. Bake for 5 minutes longer. Cool on wire rack.
- Yield: 8 to 10 dozen.

Oatmeal Molasses Cookies

$1/2$ cup shortening
$11/4$ cups sugar
$1/2$ cup molasses
2 eggs
$11/3$ cups flour
1 teaspoon salt
1 teaspoon baking soda
1 teaspoon cinnamon
2 cups quick-cooking oats
$11/2$ cups raisins

- Combine shortening, sugar, molasses and eggs in mixer bowl; beat until well blended.
- Sift flour, salt, baking soda and cinnamon together. Add to molasses mixture; mix well. Stir in oats and raisins.
- Drop by teaspoonfuls 2 inches apart onto greased cookie sheet.
- Bake at 400 degrees for 8 to 10 minutes. Watch carefully; do not wait for cookies to brown on edges or they will have a burned taste.
- Yield: 2 to 3 dozen.

Pecan Squares Americana

1 cup butter, softened
1/2 cup sugar
1 egg
1/4 teaspoon salt
Grated rind of 1 large
  lemon
3 cups sifted flour
1 cup butter, cut up
1/2 cup honey
1/4 cup sugar
1 cup plus 2 tablespoons
  packed brown sugar
1/4 cup heavy cream
5 cups pecan halves

- Butter a 10x15-inch baking pan. Place in refrigerator or freezer to chill as dough is easier to spread on cold pan.
- Beat softened butter and 1/2 cup sugar in mixer bowl just until mixed. Add egg, salt and lemon rind; beat until blended. Add flour gradually, beating just until mixture holds together.
- Drop by spoonfuls onto cold baking pan. Press with floured fingertips to cover bottom and sides of pan. Prick with fork at 1/4-inch intervals. Chill in refrigerator or freezer for 10 minutes.
- Adjust oven rack 1/3 up from bottom. Preheat oven to 375 degrees.
- Bake for 20 minutes or until lightly colored around edges. If dough puffs while baking, prick gently with fork.
- Heat 1 cup butter with honey in heavy 3-quart saucepan over medium-high heat until butter melts, stirring constantly. Add sugars; stir until sugars dissolve.
- Bring to a boil. Boil for exactly 2 minutes; do not stir. Remove from heat.
- Add heavy cream and pecan halves; mix well. Spread evenly over half-baked crust.
- Bake for 25 minutes. Let stand until completely cooled.
- Loosen from sides of baking pan. Place cookie sheet over baking pan; invert and remove pan. If topping has run through crust and caused layer to stick to pan, rap inverted pan sharply against cookie sheet to release layer onto cookie sheet.
- Cover with wire rack or another cookie sheet; invert again so that pecan layer is on top. Slide onto cutting surface. Cut into squares using long heavy knife, wiping blade frequently with damp cloth.
- Yield: 4 dozen.

GIFTS FROM THE KITCHEN

CLOCK TOWER AT OLD UNION STATION • WATERBURY

Easter Seals

Bleu Pecan Delights

5 ounces bleu cheese,
  softened
2 tablespoons butter,
  softened
2 ounces cream cheese,
  softened
48 to 60 pecan halves

- Combine bleu cheese, butter and cream cheese in food processor container. Process until smooth.
- Chill, covered, until firm.
- Place 1 teaspoon cheese mixture between 2 pecan halves. Place on cookie sheet.
- Chill, covered, until serving time.
- Yield: 24 to 30 servings.

Sugar Walnuts

1 cup sugar
1 1/2 teaspoons cinnamon
1/8 teaspoon salt
1/3 cup milk
3 cups walnut halves

- Combine sugar, cinnamon, salt and milk in saucepan; mix well. Cook until thickened, stirring constantly. Add walnuts, stirring until coated.
- Pour onto waxed paper. Cool. Store in airtight container.
- Yield: 24 servings.

Holiday Walnuts

1 pound walnut halves
2 egg whites
2 tablespoons water
2 teaspoons cinnamon
1/2 teaspoon ground cloves
1/2 teaspoon nutmeg
1/2 cup sugar

- Mix walnuts, egg whites and water in bowl. Add mixture of cinnamon, cloves, nutmeg and sugar; mix well. Spoon onto baking sheet.
- Bake at 300 degrees for 30 minutes, turning walnuts every 10 minutes.
- May substitute pecan halves for walnut halves.
- Yield: 32 servings.

Sherried Mixed Nuts

1/4 cup dry sherry
1/4 teaspoon allspice
2 tablespoons light corn
   syrup
1 (12-ounce) can salted
   mixed nuts

- Combine sherry, allspice and corn syrup in bowl; mix well. Add mixed nuts, stirring until coated. Spoon into 10-inch microwave-safe pie plate.
- Microwave on High for 6¹/₂ to 8¹/₂ minutes or until liquid is absorbed and nuts are glazed, stirring every 2 minutes.
- Spread nuts on foil-lined baking sheet. Let stand until cool.
- Store, covered, in cool dry place up to 2 weeks.
- Yield: 24 servings.

Apricot Brandy

1 (6-ounce) package dried
   apricots, chopped
1 cup sugar
1¹/₂ cups white wine
1 cup vodka

- Combine apricots, sugar and white wine in microwave-safe 4-cup bowl; mix well.
- Microwave, covered, on High for 4 to 6 minutes or until sugar dissolves and mixture comes to a boil, stirring every 2 minutes. Cool to room temperature. Skim off foam.
- Stir in vodka. Pour into bottle; seal with lid.
- Let stand in cool dark place for 1 month, shaking bottle occasionally.
- Strain into decorative bottle for gift giving.
- Yield: 1 bottle.

Crème de Menthe

1½ cups sugar
1 cup water
1½ cups vodka or gin
¼ teaspoon green food
  coloring
1 teaspoon mint extract

- Combine sugar and water in microwave-safe dish; mix well.
- Microwave on High for 4 to 5 minutes or until mixture boils. Boil for 5 minutes, stirring occasionally.
- Cool to room temperature. Skim off foam.
- Stir in vodka, green food coloring and mint extract. Pour into bottle; seal with lid.
- Let stand in cool dark place for 1 month, shaking bottle occasionally.
- Yield: 1 bottle.

Kahlua

½ cup instant coffee
1 cup hot water
3 cups sugar
⅔ cup hot water
1½ tablespoons vanilla
  extract
½ (1 fifth) grain alcohol

- Bring instant coffee and 1 cup hot water to a boil in saucepan, stirring constantly.
- Bring sugar and ⅔ cup hot water to a boil in saucepan, stirring constantly; reduce heat.
- Boil for 3 minutes. Stir in coffee mixture. Cook for 2 minutes, stirring constantly. Cool to room temperature.
- Add vanilla and grain alcohol, stirring until mixture changes to dark brown in color. Pour into ½ gallon bottle. Fill with cold water; seal with lid. Shake to mix.
- Let stand for 24 hours.
- Yield: 1 bottle.

Pickled Antipasto

1 cup water
1/2 cup Onion Garlic
  Vinegar (below) or
  cider vinegar
1 tablespoon salt
1 tablespoon oil
1/2 cup (1/4-inch slices)
  broccoli flowerets
1/2 cup Brussels sprouts,
  cut into halves
  lengthwise
1/2 cup (1/4-inch slices)
  carrots
1/2 cup (1/4-inch slices)
  cauliflowerets
1/2 cup water
1/2 cup (1-inch pieces)
  whole mushrooms
1/2 cup green or black
  olives
1/2 cup (1-inch pieces)
  green bell pepper
1/2 cup (1/4-inch slices)
  cucumber
Dill, basil or oregano sprig

- Combine 1 cup water, vinegar, salt and oil in microwave-safe dish; mix well.
- Microwave on High for 3 1/2 to 5 1/2 minutes or until mixture comes to a boil, stirring halfway through cycle.
- Combine broccoli, Brussels sprouts, carrots, cauliflower and 1/2 cup water in 2-quart microwave-safe dish.
- Microwave, covered, for 2 to 4 minutes or until color of vegetables intensifies, stirring once. Remove vegetables to colander. Rinse with cold water; drain. Add mushrooms, olives, green pepper and cucumber; mix well.
- Pack vegetables into sterilized 1-quart jar. Add sprig of dill, basil or oregano. Pour vinegar mixture over vegetables; seal with 2-piece lid.
- Chill for 2 to 3 days. Store in refrigerator up to 1 month.
- Yield: 1 (1-quart) jar.

Onion Garlic Vinegar

2 cloves of garlic
2 pearl onions
1 1/2 cups white or cider
  vinegar

- Alternate garlic and pearl onions on 6-inch wooden skewer. Place in jar. Pour vinegar over garlic and onions.
- Microwave on High for 30 seconds to 1 1/2 minutes, or until jar is warm to touch, checking every 30 seconds. Seal jar with 2-piece lid.
- Let stand in cool dark place for 2 weeks. Store in refrigerator up to 2 months.
- Yield: 1 jar.

Blueberry Rhubarb Jam

3 cups finely chopped
  rhubarb
3 cups blueberries
7 cups sugar
2 envelopes Certo

- Bring rhubarb, blueberries and sugar to a rolling boil in saucepan, stirring constantly. Boil for 1 minute. Remove from heat.
- Add Certo; mix well. Stir for 5 minutes; skim off foam.
- Ladle into hot sterilized 1-pint jars; seal with sterilized 2-piece lids.
- May use less sugar if thinner consistency is desired.
- Yield: 9 (1-pint) jars.

Zucchini Jam

6 cups ground peeled
  zucchini
Water
6 cups sugar
1/2 cup lemon juice
1 (8-ounce) can crushed
  pineapple
1 (6-ounce) package
  apricot gelatin

- Combine zucchini with a small amount of water in saucepan; mix well.
- Cook for 6 minutes or until tender, stirring frequently; drain. Stir in sugar, lemon juice and undrained pineapple.
- Cook for 6 to 10 minutes or until desired consistency, stirring frequently. Add gelatin; mix well.
- Ladle into hot sterilized jars, leaving 1/2-inch headspace; seal with 2-piece lids.
- Yield: 6 (1/2-pint) jars.

Festive Corn Salsa

1 cup fresh or frozen
   whole kernel corn,
   cooked, drained
1 papaya, cut into 1/4-inch
   pieces
1/3 cup chopped red onion
2 plum tomatoes, seeded,
   chopped
1 1/2 teaspoons minced
   garlic
1 tablespoon lime zest
1/4 cup fresh lime juice
1/3 cup chopped fresh
   cilantro

- Combine corn, papaya, red onion, tomatoes, garlic, lime zest and lime juice in bowl; mix well.
- Chill, covered, in refrigerator. Stir in cilantro just before serving.
- Yield: 32 servings.

Chunky Chili Sauce

5 (16-ounce) cans
   tomatoes
3 green bell peppers,
   chopped
3 large onions, chopped
1 large stalk celery,
   chopped
1 cup vinegar
1 1/2 cups sugar
2 tablespoons cinnamon
1 tablespoon ground
   cloves
2 teaspoons pepper
1 tablespoon salt

- Drain tomatoes, reserving juice. Chop tomatoes.
- Combine reserved juice, tomatoes, green peppers, onions, celery, vinegar and sugar in large saucepan; mix well. Bring mixture to a boil, stirring occasionally. Stir in cinnamon, cloves, pepper and salt; reduce heat.
- Simmer for 1 to 1 1/2 hours or until desired degree of consistency, stirring occasionally.
- Ladle into sterilized jars, leaving 1/2-inch headspace; seal with 2-piece lids.
- Yield: 5 (1-pint) jars.

Quick Fresh Salsa

2 cloves of garlic
1 to 4 jalapeño peppers, seeded
1 small bunch cilantro
1 medium onion, coarsely chopped
1 medium tomato, coarsely chopped
1 tablespoon olive oil
Juice of 1/2 lime
4 to 8 ounces no-salt-added tomato sauce
Salt to taste

- Combine garlic and jalapeño peppers in food processor container. Process until chopped.
- Add cilantro. Process until chopped. Add onion and tomato. Process until chopped.
- Add mixture of olive oil, lime juice, tomato sauce and salt. Process until blended.
- Serve with chips or low-fat crackers or serve as topping with fajitas and Mexican salads.
- Yield: 8 to 10 servings.

Pear Salsa

2 tablespoons coarsely chopped fresh cilantro
2 cloves of garlic
3 scallions
1 to 2 jalapeño peppers, peeled, seeded
1 Hungarian green pepper, roasted, peeled
1 red bell pepper
2 pears, peeled, cooked
1 tablespoon fresh lime juice
Salt and pepper to taste

- Combine cilantro, garlic and scallions in food processor container. Process until chopped. Add jalapeño peppers. Process until chopped. Add green pepper, red pepper and pears. Process until chopped.
- Add lime juice, salt and pepper; mix well.
- Chill for 1 hour or longer. Serve with grilled chicken or fish.
- May substitute any green pepper, except green bell pepper, for Hungarian green pepper.
- Yield: 8 to 10 servings.

CHARTS & MORE

SEAGULLS ON PILINGS • GUILFORD HARBOR

Easter
Seals

Contributors

Rosemary Abbott
Gladys Ackerman
Melinda Adams
Sally Addams
Gail Ahl
Anita Alberti
Valerie Alberti
Patti Allbritton
Erik Anderson—
    Lighthouse Inn
Mrs. William Anderson
Noreen Aresco
John Astin—aka Gomez
    from The Addams
    Family
Christelle Aube
Therese Aube
Joan Baffaro
Donna Baker
Diane Barlow
Julie Barrett—
    Connecticut
    Culinary Institute
Susan P. Barrett
Wilma L. Barrett
Sally Barter
Pam Basilicato
Victoria Bates
Paula Bauer
Betty Beaumont
Lori Beirne
Sophie Belniak
Theresa Belniak
Sharon Benard
Elizabeth Gara Berardino
John Bernache
Joan Black
Suzanne Black
Karen Blackman
Mark Blicker—
    Foxwoods
John A. Bloomquist
Margaret Bombaci
Michael Bonanno, Jr.—
    Foxwoods

Shirley & David
    Bonnheim
Marlene Bowen
Joan Boyd
Shirley Bradley
Edna Brucoli
Carole Brunell
Bill Bunin
Margaret Burns
Tracy-Lee Buturla
Maura Cahill
Lori Canney
Loraine M. Carbone
Barbara Carey
Emily Carlberg
Cathy Carley
Pat Carrano
Joanne Carroll
Catherine M. Carter
Tara Casey
Roberta Cassidy
Sally Ann Cesana
Bill Chaisson
Pam Chernovetz
Bonnie Cipriano
Sandy Civitello
Alice Clark
Calvin G. Clouser
Wendy Cloutier
Karen Coan
Lauren E. Coffey-Franco
Christine Consiglio
Barbara Conte
Dolores Conte
Laurie Coppola
Mary Cortright
Marge Coutermarsh
Ruth Cox
Jon Crane
Marlene Criscuolo
Elizabeth Cronin
Bruce Crowell
Marie Cunningham
Barbara Curreri
Cathy Curti

Myra Cusano
Bobbie Czarsty
Marietta D'Albero
Luigi D'Alessondris
Ardienne Damicis
J. P. Daniels
Amanda Danielson
David M. DeFlumeri
Jean DeMarsilis
Betsy Demir
Jean DeNicolo
Jacqueline Denton
Rita DePault
Brown Derby
Peggy DeVito
Linda Dickson
Michael Dipollino
Doris Dixon
Judy Donat
Betty Ann Donegan
Kathryn Donovan
Alex Doucette—Big Al's
Elizabeth Dougherty
Jane Dougherty
Maureen Dubuc
Lillian Dunn
Marie Durso
Colleen Dwyer
Ed Dwyer
Kerry Dwyer
Patricia Dwyer
Georgia Erickson
Florence Erlanger
Annice Estes
Sally Ewen
Dru Farquhar
Debbie Farver
Ronnie Faugno
Lynn M. Fauzio
Susan Fenaugnty
Ilda Ferrie
Lisa Film
Adele Finer
Mary T. Finn
Ellen Fitzpatrick

Helen Flanagan
Nancy Fletcher
Maureen E. Flynn
Sarah Forster
Annette Fraulo
Dorothea Fredrickson
Linda Friedlander
Ellen S. Fritz
Dawn Marie Fusco
Joanne M. Gaffney
Alcine Gager
Rita Gaj
Laura M. Gallo
Kathy Gavigan
Linda Gedeon
Michael Gibbons
Brenda Gibson
Rose A. Gilbert
Rose F. Gilmartin
Joyce Giordano
Maryann Glotzer
Kathleen Glynn
Dolores Goetz
Cindy Gonzalez
Josephine Gradwell
Marion A. Graham
Della Greenberg
Doris Greene
June Gregorski
Audrey R. Gruden
Joumana Hajj
Andrea Hamilton
Helene Handelman
Kathleen Hanning
Susan Harkins
Ann Haskins
Annette Hastings
Marlene Haverhill
Anne Healey
Mary Pat C. Healy
Kathy Heath
Melinda Hennigar
Kenneth Hervieux—
    Jamms
Susanne Heywood
Jean Hirsch
Mary Hogan
William Clay Howe

Elizabeth Hudock
Rose Hyde
Paul L. Jacques
John Jenkins
Christine Johansson
David Johnsen
Donna Marie Johnson
Donna S. Johnson
Jean Johnson
Judy Johnson
Mary Johnson
Jr. Woman's Club of
    Rocky Hill
Michael Jubinsky
Sandra Delano Jubinsky
Laura Karnauchov
Goldie Kasimer
Louise Kemler Kaufman
Lacie Kearns
Joan Kenna
Elaine Kennedy
Erin Kennedy
Patricia Kilcoyne
Faith L. Kjellson
Florence Klewin—
    Kitchen Little
Peggy Knowlton
Barbara Koren
Isabel Krasnavage
Helen Kraus
Maria Krotsis
Hulda Kugge
Joyce Carta LaBruna
Jean C. LaCamera
Shirley Lake
Jill Landon
Frances LaRosa
Caroline Larson
Harriett Lattanzi
Janice Lawrence
Dolores Leary
Esther Leary
Enid L'Heureux
Kathryn F. Lirot
Denise Lombard
Nancy Longley
Joanne M. Longo
Paula Luby

Wendy Luciani
Jean Ludwig
Evelyn Magera
Dorothy Makula
Judith Martin
Maribeth Mauri
Elizabeth Mazza
Jo-Ann Mazzadra
Kathleen McDermott
Nicole McGuire
Bridget McKenna
Emma McLauchlan
George McLauchlan
Pam McNiff
Margaret Menzies
Linda Mesite
Barbara Metz
Darlene Meyers
David Miguel
Marian Milbank
Charlotte Ming
Danielle Minkowicz
T. Michele Minteer
Rachel S. Mirabel
Judith Mirrer
Stephanie Mitchell
Linda Mizzi
Jennifer Monahan
Amy & Ray Moquet
Julia Moran
Brittany Morgan
Gerry Morrison
Scott Mueller
Karen Munson—
    Munson's Chocolates
Judith D. Murray
State Senator Amelia P.
    Mustone
Cynthia A. Nargi
Rosemary H. Nevin
Joyce Nicotera
Gail G. Nixon
Catherine Noonan
Joann F. Noonan
Jean North
Marcia Nye
Nancy Nyhan
Catherine O'Hara

Lisa Olivier
Jerry Olson
Scott Olson
Jennifer O'Neill
Mary Osborn
Adele Otis
Dorothy Otto
Anne Owens
Ann Page
Hazel L. Page
Dolores Palumbo
Nicole Pappalo
Jennifer Pappas
Barbara E. Parker
Margaret Parker
Jessica Parlato
Diane Pastore
Jennifer Patterson
Nellie Pawlak
Linda Pegnataro
Megan Peterson
Brianna Petit
Joyce Phillips
Rose Pietroniro
Linda Piscitelli
Diane Poiner
Dolores G. Pollard
Paula Pompare
Susan Ponton
Levina Powers
Sherry Proctor
Tami Pugrab
John R. Quinn
Kathy Raffone
Janet Reardon
Dorothy Reiser
Diana Renouf
Bea Reynolds
Joan Reynolds
Sally Rianhard
Jack Ribera
Mrs. Albert F. Ridinger
Carmela Rinaldi
Barbara Roberts
Peg Roberts
Margaret Robinson
Charles Roderick
Christine Roderick

Constance Roderick
Ultima Roderick
Patricia Rupp
Melissa Saccavino
Lisa Sader
Robert Sader
Penny Sampoli
Peg Sancomb
Denise B. Sansone
Jose Santiago
Ben Sauer—Foxwoods
Nancy Saunders
Carol Savageau
Pat Sawicki
Justine Scheidel
Shirley Scholder
Trudi Schott
Todd Schrager
Jane Schulze
Mrs. Frances Schwartz
Yvonne Scott
Tami B. Scotto
Doreen Scozzari
Lea D. Seabury
Robin Seabury
Elizabeth Service
Phyllis Z. Seton
Vicki A. Shepherd
Karen Siclari
Joan M. Siebert
Sharon Siegel
Rosemary Slattery
Jean Slocum
Diane Smith
JoAnn Smith
Roberta Smolskis
Jay Sneideman
Donna Snell
John Snell
Anna Sorensen
Ellen G. Spring
Diana Stadtmiller
Patricia Stafford
Jean Stasiewski
Donna Stephens
Nora Stewart
Kurt Stiles—
    Moosehopper Cafe

Leslie Strauss
Mafaldo Summers
Khristine Sutton—Two
    Sisters Deli
April Sweeney
Elsie "Biz" Swensson
Mary Tarca
Penny Thorpe
Marcia Tighe
Stella Tobin
Julia Toohey
Rachel Trent
Jennifer Trumpold
Valerie Tudan
J. Madeline Tunucci—
    Connecticut
    Culinary Institute
Sandra Ulrich
Claudia Upham
Rozann Valenti
Beth Vickery
Maria Vincenzo
Marilyn Wagner
Wendy Waller
Ruth Walsh
Kathie Walters
Susan Ward
Karen Watkins
Terri Webber
Sharon West
Claire M. Whalley
Henrietta Whelan
Charlotte White
Barbara Whitney
Larry Willette
Barbara R. Williams
Thomasina Willman
Jean Winch
Kathy Winchester
Windsor Jr. Women's
    Club
Ann Wollenberg
Madeline Yaccarino
Joe Zaccagnino
Paul Zenga—Mystic
    Hilton

Substitution Chart

	Instead of	Use
Baking	1 teaspoon baking powder	1/4 teaspoon baking soda plus 1/2 teaspoon cream of tartar
	1 tablespoon cornstarch (for thickening)	2 tablespoons all-purpose flour or 1 tablespoon tapioca
	1 cup sifted all-purpose flour	1 cup plus 2 tablespoons sifted cake flour
	1 cup sifted cake flour	1 cup minus 2 tablespoons sifted all-purpose flour
	1 cup dry bread crumbs	3/4 cup cracker crumbs
Dairy	1 cup buttermilk	1 cup sour milk or 1 cup yogurt
	1 cup heavy cream	3/4 cup skim milk plus 1/3 cup butter
	1 cup light cream	7/8 cup skim milk plus 3 tablespoons butter
	1 cup sour cream	7/8 cup sour milk plus 3 tablespoons butter
	1 cup sour milk	1 cup milk plus 1 tablespoon vinegar or lemon juice or 1 cup buttermilk
Seasoning	1 teaspoon allspice	1/2 teaspoon cinnamon plus 1/8 teaspoon ground cloves
	1 cup catsup	1 cup tomato sauce plus 1/2 cup sugar plus 2 tablespoons vinegar
	1 clove of garlic	1/8 teaspoon garlic powder or 1/8 teaspoon instant minced garlic or 3/4 teaspoon garlic salt
	1 teaspoon Italian spice	1/4 teaspoon each oregano, basil, thyme, rosemary plus dash of cayenne pepper
	1 teaspoon lemon juice	1/2 teaspoon vinegar
	1 tablespoon mustard	1 teaspoon dry mustard
	1 medium onion	1 tablespoon dried minced onion or 1 teaspoon onion powder
Sweet	1 1-ounce square chocolate	1/4 cup baking cocoa plus 1 teaspoon shortening
	1 2/3 ounces semisweet chocolate	1 ounce unsweetened chocolate plus 4 teaspoons granulated sugar
	1 cup honey	1 to 1 1/4 cups sugar plus 1/4 cup liquid or 1 cup corn syrup or molasses
	1 cup granulated sugar	1 cup packed brown sugar or 1 cup corn syrup, molasses or honey minus 1/4 cup liquid

Equivalent Chart

	When the recipe calls for	Use
Baking	½ cup butter 2 cups butter 4 cups all-purpose flour 4½ to 5 cups sifted cake flour 1 square chocolate 1 cup semisweet chocolate chips 4 cups marshmallows 2¼ cups packed brown sugar 4 cups confectioners' sugar 2 cups granulated sugar	4 ounces 1 pound 1 pound 1 pound 1 ounce 6 ounces 1 pound 1 pound 1 pound 1 pound
Cereal – Bread	1 cup fine dry bread crumbs 1 cup soft bread crumbs 1 cup small bread cubes 1 cup fine cracker crumbs 1 cup fine graham cracker crumbs 1 cup vanilla wafer crumbs 1 cup crushed cornflakes 4 cups cooked macaroni 3½ cups cooked rice	4 to 5 slices 2 slices 2 slices 28 saltines 15 crackers 22 wafers 3 cups uncrushed 8 ounces uncooked 1 cup uncooked
Dairy	1 cup shredded cheese 1 cup cottage cheese 1 cup sour cream 1 cup whipped cream ⅔ cup evaporated milk 1⅔ cups evaporated milk	4 ounces 8 ounces 8 ounces ½ cup heavy cream 1 small can 1 13-ounce can

Fruit	4 cups sliced or chopped apples
	1 cup mashed bananas
	2 cups pitted cherries
	2½ cups shredded coconut
	4 cups cranberries
	1 cup pitted dates
	1 cup candied fruit
	3 to 4 tablespoons lemon juice plus
	  1 tablespoon grated lemon rind
	⅓ cup orange juice plus 2 tablespoons
	  grated orange rind
	4 cups sliced peaches
	2 cups pitted prunes
	3 cups raisins
		4 medium
		3 medium
		4 cups unpitted
		8 ounces
		1 pound
		1 8-ounce package
		1 8-ounce package
		1 lemon
		
		1 orange
		
		8 medium
		1 12-ounce package
		1 15-ounce package

When the recipe calls for	Use
Meats 4 cups chopped cooked chicken 3 cups chopped cooked meat 2 cups cooked ground meat	1 5-pound chicken 1 pound, cooked 1 pound, cooked
Nuts 1 cup chopped nuts	4 ounces shelled 1 pound unshelled
Vegetables 2 cups cooked green beans 2½ cups lima beans or red beans 4 cups shredded cabbage 1 cup grated carrot 8 ounces fresh mushrooms 1 cup chopped onion 4 cups sliced or chopped potatoes 2 cups canned tomatoes	½ pound fresh or 1 16-ounce can 1 cup dried, cooked 1 pound 1 large 1 4-ounce can 1 large 4 medium 1 16-ounce can

Measurement Equivalents

1 tablespoon = 3 teaspoons
2 tablespoons = 1 ounce
4 tablespoons = ¼ cup
5⅓ tablespoons = ⅓ cup
8 tablespoons = ½ cup
12 tablespoons = ¾ cup
16 tablespoons = 1 cup
1 cup = 8 ounces or ½ pint
4 cups = 1 quart
4 quarts = 1 gallon

1   6½ to 8-ounce can = 1 cup
1   10½ to 12-ounce can = 1¼ cups
1   14 to 16-ounce can = 1¾ cups
1   16 to 17-ounce can = 2 cups
1   18 to 20-ounce can = 2½ cups
1   29-ounce can = 3½ cups
1   46 to 51-ounce can = 5¾ cups
1   6½ to 7½-pound can or
Number 10 = 12 to 13 cups

Metric Equivalents

Liquid	Dry
1 teaspoon = 5 milliliters 1 tablespoon = 15 milliliters 1 fluid ounce = 30 milliliters 1 cup = 250 milliliters 1 pint = 500 milliliters	1 quart = 1 liter 1 ounce = 30 grams 1 pound = 450 grams 2.2 pounds = 1 kilogram

NOTE: The metric measures are approximate benchmarks for purposes of home food preparation.

Cheese Chart

CHEESE	GOES WITH	USED FOR	FLAVOR, TEXTURE
Bel Paese (Italy)	Fresh fruit French bread	Dessert Snack	Spongy, mild, creamy yellow interior
Bleu (France)	Fresh fruit Bland crackers	Dessert Dips, Salads	Marbled, blue-veined, semisoft, piquant
Brie (France)	Fresh fruit	Dessert Snack	Soft, edible crust, creamy
Brick (U.S.)	Crackers Bread	Sandwiches Snack	Semisoft, mild, cream-colored to orange
Camembert (France)	Apples	Dessert Snack	Mild to pungent, edible crust, yellow
Cheddar (England)	Fresh fruit Crackers	Dessert Cooking, Snack	Mild to sharp, cream-colored to orange
Cottage (U.S.)	Canned or Fresh fruit	Fruit salads Cooking	Soft, moist, mild, white
Cream (U.S.)	Crackers and Jelly	Dessert, Cooking Sandwiches	Soft, smooth, mild, white
Edam (Holland)	Fresh fruit	Dessert Snack	Firm, mild, red wax coating
Feta (Greece)	Greek salad	Salad Cooking	Salty, crumbly, white
Gorgonzola (Italy)	Fresh fruit Italian bread	Dessert Snack	Semisoft, blue-veined, piquant
Gouda (Holland)	Fresh fruit Crackers	Dessert Snack	Softer than Edam, mild, nutty

Cheese Chart

CHEESE	GOES WITH	USED FOR	FLAVOR, TEXTURE
Gruyère (Switzerland)	Fresh fruit	Dessert Fondue	Nutty, bland, firm, tiny holes
Liederkranz (Germany)	Onion slices Dark bread	Dessert Snack	Edible light orange crust, robust, soft
Limburger (Belgium)	Dark bread Bland crackers	Dessert	Soft, smooth, white, robust, aromatic
Mozzarella (Italy)	Italian foods	Cooking Pizza	Semisoft, delicate, mild, white
Muenster (Germany)	Crackers Bread	Sandwiches Snack	Semisoft, mild to mellow
Parmesan (Italy)	Italian foods	Cooking	Hard, brittle, sharp, light yellow
Port Salut (France)	Fresh fruit Crackers	Dessert Snack	Buttery, semisoft
Provolone (Italy)	Italian foods	Cooking Dessert	Salty, smoky, mild to sharp, hard
Ricotta (Italy)	Italian foods	Cooking Fillings	Soft, creamy, bland, white
Roquefort (France)	Bland crackers Fresh fruit	Dips, Salads Dessert	Semisoft, sharp, blue-veined, crumbly
Stilton (England)	Fresh fruit Bland crackers	Dips, Salads Dessert	Semisoft, sharp, blue-veined
Swiss (Switzerland)	Fresh fruit French bread	Cooking, Snack Sandwiches	Sweetish, nutty, holes, pale yellow

Cheeses from Around the World

Cheese is one of the oldest foods known to man and has appeared in some form wherever he has grazed animals and used their milk. The Persian philosopher, Zoroaster, is reputed to have lived for 20 years on cheese alone in the 6th century. Cheese is frequently mentioned in the Bible. The famous Gorgonzola cheese has been made in the Po Valley in Italy since 879 A.D., and the great monasteries of Europe were well known for cheese-making throughout the Middle Ages. Since that time, each country and region of the world has developed cheeses which are an integral part of their cooking and are readily identified with the cuisine of the country.

Cheese is a universal and almost-perfect food. It contains many of the essential food elements which the body needs, such as proteins, fats and vitamins. The rich variety of tastes makes it appealing to everyone—with the choice depending primarily on how it is to be used.

The milk from which cheese is made is separated into whey and curd. It is generally the curd which is pressed, treated, and ripened into cheese. The two main types of cheese are *natural* cheese and *pasteurized* process cheese products.

Natural cheeses are made by different methods; this accounts for their varying characteristics. Cheeses produced by the same method are grouped as a "family," and although textures and sharpness vary, the flavors within a family are basically similar. The nine basic cheese families are: Cheddar, Dutch, Provolone, Swiss, Bleu, Parmesan, Fresh, Surface-ripened and Whey. Natural cheeses may also be classified by texture or consistency: hard-grating, such as Parmesan; hard, such as Cheddar and Swiss; semisoft, such as Brick and Bel Paese; soft, such as Brie and Limburger; and soft, unripened, such as cottage cheese and ricotta.

Pasteurized process cheese is made by grinding and blending one or more natural cheeses of varying strengths, then heating or pasteurizing it with an emulsifier to stop further ripening and produce cheese of uniform, consistent flavor.

The important thing to remember when cooking with cheese is that excessive heat and prolonged cooking cause it to become stringy and leathery. High heat may also cause a mixture of cheese, eggs and milk to curdle. When making a sauce, add the cheese toward the end of the cooking time, stirring over low heat just long enough to melt and blend it with the other ingredients. A cheese topping should be broiled several inches away from the heat source. Casseroles with cheese should be baked at low to medium temperatures.

One pound of shredded cheese will measure four cups for use in recipes. One pound of soft cheese such as cottage cheese or cream cheese will measure two cups.

Index

Classic Connecticut Cuisine

Easter Seals
P.O. Box 100, 147 Jones Street
Hebron, Connecticut 06248
1-800-874-7687

Please send _____ copies of **Classic Connecticut Cuisine** at $14.95 plus $3.00 for shipping and handling per book. Connecticut residents add 6% state sales tax ($1.08 per book).

Total copies @ $19.03 _____   Total amount enclosed $ _____

MasterCard or VISA #: _____   Exp. Date: _____

Signature _____

Name _____

Address_____

City_____ State _____ Zip _____

Make checks payable to Easter Seals.

Classic Connecticut Cuisine

Easter Seals
P.O. Box 100, 147 Jones Street
Hebron, Connecticut 06248
1-800-874-7687

Please send _____ copies of **Classic Connecticut Cuisine** at $14.95 plus $3.00 for shipping and handling per book. Connecticut residents add 6% state sales tax ($1.08 per book).

Total copies @ $19.03 _____   Total amount enclosed $ _____

MasterCard or VISA #: _____   Exp. Date: _____

Signature _____

Name _____

Address_____

City_____ State _____ Zip _____

Make checks payable to Easter Seals.

See reverse side for gift card information.

Classic Connecticut Cuisine

(   ) Please enclose a gift card to read:

_____

_____

_____

_____

All copies of **Classic Connecticut Cuisine** will be sent to same address unless otherwise specified. If you wish one or more books sent as gifts, furnish a list of names and addresses of recipients. If you wish to enclose your own gift card with each book, please write name of recipient on outside of the envelope, enclose with order, and we will include it with your gift.

Classic Connecticut Cuisine

(   ) Please enclose a gift card to read:

_____

_____

_____

_____

All copies of **Classic Connecticut Cuisine** will be sent to same address unless otherwise specified. If you wish one or more books sent as gifts, furnish a list of names and addresses of recipients. If you wish to enclose your own gift card with each book, please write name of recipient on outside of the envelope, enclose with order, and we will include it with your gift.